Nation-building

D1354955

Nation-building

A Key Concept for Peaceful Conflict Transformation?

Edited by Jochen Hippler

Translated by Barry Stone

Pluto Press

LONDON • ANN ARBOR, MI

In association with the
Development and Peace Foundation, Bonn

First published in German 2004 as *Nation-Building – Ein Schlüsselkonzept für friedliche Konfliktbearbeitung?*, by Verlag J.H.W. Dietz Nachf. GmbH, Bonn

First published in English 2005 by Pluto Press
345 Archway Road, London N6 5AA
and 839 Greene Street, Ann Arbor, MI 48106

www.plutobooks.com

Published with the support of the German Ministry for Economic Cooperation and Development.

British Library Cataloguing in Publication Data
A catalogue record for this book is available from the British Library

ISBN   0 7453 2336 7 hardback
ISBN   0 7453 2335 9 paperback

Library of Congress Cataloging in Publication Data applied for

10   9   8   7   6   5   4   3   2   1

Designed and produced for Pluto Press by
Chase Publishing Services Ltd, Fortescue, Sidmouth, EX10 9QG, England
Typeset from disk by Stanford DTP Services, Northampton, England
Printed and bound in the European Union by
Antony Rowe Ltd, Chippenham and Eastbourne, England

Contents

Part II   Case Studies

List of Abbreviations

ACA	Afghan Assistance Coordination Authority
APA	Afghanistan Peace Association
AU	African Union
CARDS	Community Assistance for Reconstruction, Development and Stabilisation
CIA	Central Intelligence Agency
CIMIC	civil-military cooperation
EAC	East African Community
ECOWAS	Economic Community of West African States
EU	European Union
FES	Friedrich Ebert Foundation
Frelimo	Frente de Libertação de Moçambique (Mozambican Liberation Front)
ICRC	International Committee of the Red Cross
IGAD	Intergovernmental Authority on Development
IMF	International Monetary Fund
ISAF	International Security Assistance Force Afghanistan
KAS	Konrad Adenauer Foundation
KDP	Kurdish Democratic Party
KFOR	Kosovo Force (NATO)
LPI	Life and Peace Institute, Sweden
MIFTAH	Palestinian Initiative for the Promotion of Global Dialogue and Democracy
OAU	Organisation of African Unity
OECD	Organisation for Economic Co-operation and Development
OSCE	Organization for Security and Co-operation in Europe
NATO	North Atlantic Treaty Organisation
NGOs	non-governmental organisations
PUK	Patriotic Union Kurdistan
Renamo	Resistência Nacional Moçambicana (Mozambican National Resistance)
SADC	Southern African Development Community
SAP	Stabilisation and Association Process
SCIRI	Supreme Council for Islamic Revolution in Iraq
SEF	Development and Peace Foundation, Bonn
SLORC	State Law and Order Restoration Council, Myanmar

SPDC	State Peace and Development Council (previously SLORC), Myanmar
SRP	Somalia Rehabilitation Programme
TANU	Tanganyika African National Union
TNG	transitional national government
UÇK	Kosovo Liberation Army
UN	United Nations
UNDP	United Nations Development Programme
UNMIK	United Nations Interim Administration Mission in Kosovo
UNOSOM	United Nations Operation in Somalia
UNTAC	United Nations Transitional Authority in Cambodia
US	United States of America
USDA	Union Solidarity and Development Association, Myanmar
USIP	United States Institute of Peace

Preface

The conquests of Afghanistan and Iraq and the attempts to establish new state systems there have caused the term 'nation-building' to become so popular that it is now even used by ministers and heads of governments. In a time characterised by economic and political globalisation plus, at the same time, numerous ethnic conflicts, failing and failed states, humanitarian interventions, peace-keeping operations and 'liberal protectorates' (Ignatieff), the question of building new nation-states is taking on exceptional importance.

Nation-building has occupied an important place in the debate on foreign, security and development policy since the failed intervention in Somalia. Today, the term is used in the context of regional stabilisation, imperial control, conflict management and prevention, as well as development policy without its specific meaning being clarified in each case.

This book hopes to contribute towards broadening and systematising our understanding of nation-building processes. The processes of social and political fragmentation and reintegration are not only of crucial importance for promoting stability in potential conflict regions; they are also essential for avoiding and overcoming violent conflict.

The first part of the book is a compilation of chapters dealing with the general and conceptional problems of nation-building. This is followed by an analysis of important case examples from Africa, the Near and Middle East, and the Balkans. The third part then focuses on questions of dealing with nation-building in political terms.

The editor would like to thank all the authors for their fruitful and kind cooperation. This book would hardly have been possible without them and the positive cooperation of the Development and Peace Foundation (SEF) in Bonn, Germany. My gratitude, in particular, to Michèle Roth, the Foundation's Executive Director, Burkhard Könitzer, and Thomas Siebold. I would also like to thank the German Ministry for Economic Cooperation and Development for supporting the English edition of this book.

Jochen Hippler
Duisburg, March 2005

Part I

Concepts and Theoretical Aspects of Nation-building

I

Violent Conflicts, Conflict Prevention and Nation-building – Terminology and Political Concepts

Jochen Hippler

A large number of foreign policy discussions since the end of the East–West conflict have been determined by a series of regional conflicts – in addition to the dissolution and restructuring processes in the former Eastern bloc. Those that have stood out most include Iraq (Gulf War 1991, Iraq War 2003), Somalia, the wars during the breakup of the former Yugoslavia (particularly in Bosnia and Kosovo), Afghanistan, plus the wars and violent excesses in Africa (Rwanda, Burundi, Congo, Liberia and others). The perspective had been shifting since the early 1990s because it was no longer possible to squeeze each conflict into the simple schema of the Cold War. The internal causes of conflict came more to the fore, with new modes appearing, such as culturalistic interpretations (clash of civilisations) or knee-jerk ascriptions to 'ethnic' causes. In addition to other concepts – for example that of failed states – the term 'nation-building' emerged more and more in the Anglo-Saxon debate, in particular. This was noticeable in the political discussion, e.g. in the case of former US Secretary of State Alexander Haig and UN Secretary-General Boutros-Ghali (Haig 1994; UN Chronicle 1994), in the media, e.g. *Newsweek* and the *Frankfurter Allgemeine Zeitung* (*FAZ* 1994; *Newsweek* 1994), as well as in scientific analysis, e.g. through the work of Eriksen (1993) and Lenhart (1992). At the beginning, there was frequent discussion concerning the processes and problems of nation-building or its failure, though the term itself was avoided. In the meantime, the term has been used more and more, but hardly explained or addressed in theoretical terms.

In the second half of the 1990s, the term 'nation-building' gained acceptance on a broad front and became a natural part of both the political and scientific debate. The experience of the international community in places like Somalia, the Balkans, Afghanistan and Iraq made it clear that breakdown of the state and the fragmentation of societies can trigger violent conflicts or make them insoluble. Such situations can, in the longer term, cause economic, social and political development to fail, give rise to major humanitarian disasters, destabilise entire regions and even turn them into sources of transnational terrorism – also generally affecting distant countries and calling Western political objectives into question. It is especially in these contexts that nation-building is discussed at international level: either as a preventive political option to avoid the breakup of the state and social fragmentation, as an alternative to military conflict management, as part of military interventions or as an element of post-conflict policies. Accordingly, a policy of nation-building constitutes a hinge between foreign, development and military policy for the purpose of preventing or managing violent conflicts, achieving local and regional stability, and facilitating development.

Nation-building is, however, neither easy nor without problems. The chances of achieving this objective from the outside are assessed very differently and often with scepticism; the paths and instruments to success are frequently unclear and it is questionable in many instances whether external players will be able to stay the course long enough in terms of time and financial commitment. External nation-building can drag outside players into local power struggles from which they find it very difficult to extricate themselves. Questions of legality are also difficult to answer in many cases because, although the principle of non-interference under the UN Charter is often ignored, it does still exist – and for good reason. Finally, it is frequently not clear what nation-building is actually supposed to mean.

NATION-BUILDING: EARLIER DISCUSSIONS

'Nation-building' is an old term that has already flourished and declined. Nation-building was a key concept of foreign, security and development policy in the 1950s and 1960s, in particular. At that time, it was closely related to the modernisation theories fashionable during those years, which viewed the development process in the Third World in terms of catching up with Western models. Societies were to be 'modernised', that is their structures adapted to the industrialised countries through 'traditional' or 'tribal' societies being turned into 'modern' nation-states, with the European model implicitly or explicitly intended as the goal.

Nationality and the nation-state were fundamental categories, with economic and political development regarded as promising success only in this context. In Rivkin's words (1969:156) relating to Africa:

> Nation-building and economic development ... are twin goals and intimately related tasks, sharing many of the same problems, confronting many of the same challenges, and interrelating at many levels of public policy and practice.

Economic development was perceived to imply a market economy, and political development a nation-state. Political development as a component of or prerequisite for economic development was thus regarded above all as a nation-building process. The two together, that is accomplishment of the market mechanism and the nation-state, were regarded as being closely linked and as 'modernisation'.

It is evident that this view of 'development' – modernisation, nation-state and nation-building – applied European experiences to the Third World in a rather schematic manner. In some cases, Western state-building processes were even reappraised in explicit terms in order to learn lessons for nation-building in the Third World (after Lipset 1963).

Nation-building also took place in the 1950s and 1960s in the context of the East–West conflict and constituted a Western strategy for containing socialism and the Soviet Union in the Third World. In the same way as other concepts, it was intended to represent an alternative to the victory of liberation movements and the 'revolution'. Looking back, the head of the US development agency USAID, Brian Atwood (1994:11), summed this up in the following terms:

> Thirty years ago, nation building was largely a postcolonial phenomenon, an ambitious program to help newly independent countries acquire the institutions, infrastructure, economy, and social cohesion of more advanced nations. Nation building was a strategic and competitive enterprise, part of the Cold War competition between the United States and the Soviet Union.

The term 'nation-building' almost vanished into oblivion during the 1970s. Compromised by the constant emphasis on it in the Vietnam War, its association with military strategies and its conceptional link with markedly brutal political forms of 'pacifying' the country, it became unfashionable both politically and academically. As already pointed out, it was not until a generation later that it found favour again by being revived – first more by accident and then systematically

– in the context of complex violent conflicts, especially where these displayed strong ethnic dimensions or elements of the breakdown of the state.

CLARIFICATION OF THE CONCEPT

The term 'nation-building' is used today in a markedly vague and inconsistent manner. To simplify matters, we can distinguish between several uses of the term, which are either directed at the real course, description or analysis of (past or present) historical-social processes or are normatively oriented and focus on a system of objectives or political strategies (Hippler 2002). The two frequently overlap in day-to-day usage.

- Nation-building is, on the one hand, *a process of sociopolitical development*, which ideally – usually over a longer historical time span – allows initially loosely linked communities to become a common society with a nation-state corresponding to it. Such a process can get off the ground as a result of political, economic, social, cultural and other dynamics. However, it is not automatic that such nation-building processes will proceed successfully. They can involve extremely different dimensions and instruments, such as economic integration, cultural integration, political centralisation, bureaucratic control, military conquest or subjugation, creation of common interests, democratisation and establishment of common citizenship or repression and acts of 'ethnic cleansing'.

  There have been rather peaceful and particularly bloody nation-building processes, both in Europe and the Third World. They are thus not peaceful or conducive to constructive conflict management per se, nor are they necessarily violent. These processes combine 'natural' developments of an economic, political or cultural nature which can hardly be controlled by individual players with strategic decisions and active politics of key players who incorporate the developments for which they are not answerable and take advantage of them for themselves.

- Nation-building can, on the other hand, be *a political objective as well as a strategy* for reaching specific political objectives. Internal or external players strive to create or strengthen a political and social system constituted under a nation-state where this appears to serve their interests, where it fulfils particular functional requirements to a greater degree than a previously existing arrangement, or where it strengthens their power or weakens that of their opponents.

In such a context, the term 'nation-building' has a programmatic or conceptional character rather than serving to describe or analyse social and political processes. Either internal players strive to assert nation-state models of power or external players pursue the same objective. In both cases, this can ensue for functional reasons, such as improving social stability or economic development opportunities, though also in order to gain dominance and control in the relevant society. Nation-building can therefore be a development or imperial strategy depending on the political circumstances and players concerned.

Both variants of usage of the term 'nation-building', that is the descriptive or analytical vs the normative-strategic, are very multifaceted and heterogeneous. This is especially evident in the second form, given that nation-building can be handled very differently in strategic terms as far as the specific objectives, players, instruments and results are concerned. For this reason, the two uses of the term not only imply differing views of the same subject, they also comprise very different dimensions with regard to the time factor, mechanisms and results. However, there are certain core elements in all nation-building processes without which the process could hardly proceed successfully over the long term.

ELEMENTS OF NATION-BUILDING

A distinction can be drawn between three central elements of successful nation-building, which are closely interlinked in most cases: a unifying, persuasive ideology, integration of society and a functional state apparatus.

- Nation-building will only be successful in the long term if it stems from an *integrative ideology* or produces this from a certain point on. Fundamental restructuring of politics and society requires special legitimation with regard to justification of policy as well as social mobilisation for its ends. The different variations of 'nationalism' clearly have to be regarded as the classic ideology of nation-building – with 'nationalism' here meaning everything ranging from the meaningful development of a common national identity up to and even including violent disassociation from other national or ethnic groups. Nation-building necessarily presupposes the forming of a 'nation', which can, however, be constituted in extremely different ways. As long as people in a region define themselves *primarily* as Pashtuns, Maronites, Bavarians, Yussufzai (a Pashtun tribe), Ismailites or members of a particular clan, nation-building has either not been concluded or has failed. The existence of the respective identities is not in itself the problem but, rather, their relationship with a 'national' identity covering all groups.[1] It is quite possible for someone to be a Pakistani or Afghan *and* a Pashtun or Shiite at the same time if the two are made possible ideologically, just as someone can simultaneously be a Bavarian, Muslim and German. However, as long as the primary identity and loyalty lies with the tribe, clan or an ethnic or ethnoreligious group and the 'national' identity level remains subordinate or is missing, a nation-state will continue to be precarious. It is not absolutely essential, though, for such an integrating ideology forming the basis for nation-building to always and automatically be 'nationally' oriented. It can also be replaced by other value and identity models, at least for a time: constitutional patriotism – 'liberty, equality, fraternity' – secular ideologies (for example socialism) or religion can assume the same function or auxiliary functions. The cases of the founding of the states of Pakistan and Israel are illustrative in this respect: when states were founded for the 'Muslims of India' and 'the Jews', these originally religious classifications were increasingly reinterpreted in a 'national' way.

The second prerequisite for a successful nation-building process involves the *integration of a society* from the loosely associated groups that existed previously. Pashtuns, Baluchis and Punjabis must not only be convinced that they belong to a common nation, this notion must also be founded in the social reality. To achieve this, the patterns of communication *between* the social groups need to be intensified to the extent that communication does not principally take place within the groups. Even though the internal communication of the (ethnic, religious and other) groups may remain stronger than that between them, a certain degree of close communication among them is a requirement for successful and enduring nation-building. However, apart from the political-cultural aspect, there are also practical requirements for this: nation-building needs a 'national' infrastructure. Transport and communication infrastructures, the development of a 'national economy' from regional or local economic areas, plus nationwide mass media for establishing a national political and cultural discourse are key variables.

- A crucial component of nation-building is the development of a *functional state apparatus* that can actually control its national territory. This implies, firstly, that the corresponding society has constituted itself as a political society, which corresponds to the two processes outlined above, especially the formation of a common society with its own self-awareness. In this way, the state becomes the political organisational form of a society that is able to act – if it did not already exist before playing a key role in the social integration process. *State-building* is a core aspect of successful nation-building. It presupposes a range of practical capabilities, such as creating a financial basis for a functioning state apparatus, that is an effective fiscal system, as well as an organised police and legal system and an administrative apparatus that are effective and accepted throughout the country. The state needs loyal personnel that do not identify primarily with individual social, ethnic or religious communities but, rather, with the state and the 'nation'. In particular, the state apparatus must assert its monopoly of force over the entire national territory in order to be successful over the long term.

For successful nation-building, this results, altogether, in a triangle formed from the highly complex individual elements of state-building, social integration and ideological legitimation. Certain components can be provided relatively easily from outside, such as parts of the infrastructure, while others are very difficult or even impossible to furnish from outside, as in the case of ideological nation-building. In the end, however, it is only engagement with each other, providing mutual strength, that will decide the success or failure of nation-building. As a rule, external players will consequently make nation-building easier or harder, but hardly ever be able to force it or completely prevent it where the internal factors stand in the way of this.

NATION, STATE AND SOCIAL MOBILISATION

The core political elements of nation-building comprise the nation-state plus a high level of social mobilisation and political integration. The state is not the central element solely by virtue of its modern, nation-state form being one of the most important results of nation-building; it is also the decisive player for the most part.

Contrary to the view prevailing in Germany since the Age of German Romanticism that a nation exists a priori and must – or should – eventually be constituted in a state, most historical processes have been considerably more complex and frequently even gone in the opposite direction. 'Nations' do not just exist, rather they emerge like many other social phenomena in a difficult and inconsistent process – or simply do not. And in most countries, the existence of a state preceded that of a nation, even in the classic examples of European nation-states like France and England (Greenfeld 1992). For merely practical reasons, it was not rare for a state apparatus to create, intentionally or rather incidentally, a nation corresponding to itself: the old monarchies were hardly ever based on ethnic or national borders but, instead, on religious or charismatic legitimation mechanisms and compulsion. They adopted their later form through conquest or marriage with other ruling houses and not through any defined right of self-determination of the nations, which did not yet exist. And it was only via what were often long historical processes that the state apparatuses, which were becoming stronger and more bureaucratic, were able to form a nation from diverse social groups, e.g. through repression of local rulers, legal regulation of social relations and the fiscal system increasingly affecting everyone, the pressure of homogeneity for a common religion and, later, through nationwide education systems or general military conscription.

In many multiethnic (proto)societies, the impetus for pushing through social integration and creating a nation-state came and comes from the state apparatus itself, using methods like material incentives (financial, economic, public service employment etc.), cultural means (language policy, education system, policy on religion) or compulsion. In many cases, there was and is a link between internal and external causes in this regard, such as the attempt of a weak or rudimentary government to consolidate its position in its own society (and extend its tax base or repress local power factors) and to be able to better overcome foreign policy challenges, especially those of a military nature. The interest in having a fiscal system independent of the local nobility or warlords plus a well-organised and powerful military has represented a particularly important impetus for developing and relegitimising systematised state apparatuses. In this sense, most cases of nation-building would have been dominated from the top down rather than the nation-state evolving naturally from society. And, almost always, this type of state-induced nation-building has given rise to complex dialectics between the state apparatus and social groups (as well as between different parts of the state apparatus and between different social groups).

At the same time, nation-building has always signified a process of social mobilisation, either from the bottom up or from the top down. This especially applies to the constituting phase in many instances. The ideological and political process of the shaping of a nation implies its members being involved in its politics, with large numbers of people entering into the political sphere. While politics – and therefore power – was reserved for a small group or stratum of privileged persons over long periods of history and the population was the object of politics, this situation is undergoing fundamental change. The constitution of a 'nation' means that ideologically (in principle) all its members now first become political subjects instead of being subservient and tolerant of the politics of the rulers. In this sense, nation-building takes on a democratic potential because belonging to the nation is defined by citizenship or common ethnic-national interests rather than by noble birth or religious position. The power now no longer lies, at least as far as is claimed, with a king chosen by the grace of God but, rather, with the newly constituted society. The fact that it does not necessarily have to exercise what is in principle its sovereignty in a democratic way and can often be organised in a clientelistic, elitist and dictatorial manner is most regrettable, but changes nothing with regard to the legitimatory bond between power and the 'nation', i.e. what is at least claimed to be an all-inclusive community. Nation-building thus opens up democratic *potential*, but not necessarily the door to actual democracy; on the contrary, power 'in the name' of the nation can be more repressive than feudalism or the doctrine of divine right, not to mention 'traditional' forms of rule.

Nation-building therefore makes the members of a nation political subjects in principle, even if the exercising of participatory rights is often denied in reality. Nation-building 'politicises' the population into a nation, mobilising broad sections of society in the constituting process, in particular. This mostly implies specific social prerequisites, for example presupposing a significant degree of communication within the society, which is aided, in turn, by a high level of literacy and appropriate mass and communication media (in certain phases of history this was the invention of printing and, later, newspapers, radio and television).

The process of constituting the nation plus the greater participation of and ability to politically mobilise the population that has become the 'nation' does, however, mean that conflicts previously lying dormant in the society and which had little chance of being articulated by virtue of the population being excluded from politics can be effectively intensified. This is all the more true if the determination of who actually belongs to the 'nation' has not been settled or is disputed, especially in multiethnic or multireligious societies that cannot agree on common citizenship as a community criterion. If belonging to the nation is to be determined according to language, ethnic origin or religion rather than on the basis of civil equality, this can easily have two problematic consequences. First, there is a danger that ethnicising the political discourse in the context of latent conflicts and social mobilisation will lower the threshold for violence and trigger violent conflicts which are ethnically structured. Secondly, such a context transforms the nation-building process: instead of striving for or achieving the integration of society as a whole, the alternative then arises of conducting nation-building either as a repressive project of hegemony by one ethnic group over others or bringing about a situation of competition between different nation-building projects conducted by the various ethnic groups. Both lead to the intensification of existing conflicts and the risk of these being waged in a violent manner in the future.

Each nation-building process involves the creation of new political and social structures and mechanisms while overcoming and destroying old ones at the same time. For this reason, it is always and necessarily associated with the redistribution of power. Nation-building has winners and losers in political, economic and social terms – so it can also be used as a means of obtaining advantages for one's own political or social group.

Pushing through a central government where there were perhaps only regional or local rulers or extensively autonomous rural communities beforehand and bureaucratically regulating a political system formerly based on personal ties, clientelistic relations or charismatic rule are not simply elements of a more technical 'modernisation' of social structures; rather they represent a redistribution of power which is perceived as positive by some groups and as a threat by others. Nation-building is thus always a contentious process, fought out in a political, cultural, social, economic or military setting. As soon as a society in this situation is divided in ethnic or religious terms besides the economic, social and other lines of conflict, a further dimension is added to the existing potential for conflict, which can then intensify the course of the conflict as well as give it a completely new structure. Distribution and power conflicts can, for example, be ideologised in an ethnoreligious way, which further increases the degree of social mobilisation and makes pragmatic solutions more difficult. This also applies, of course, to cases where nation-building is attempted principally as a strategy by external players. Regardless of whether their intentions are of a humanitarian or imperial nature, in the target country nation-building has to bring about passive or active resistance and a shift in the balance of power.

NATION-BUILDING AS A CONCEPT

When nation-building is discussed nowadays as an element of crisis prevention and a means of post-conflict policies, the general mechanisms, experiences and problems relating to nation-building should not be ignored. It goes without saying that stable, functioning nation-states can, compared with fragmenting societies and failing states, better provide for the security of their citizens, as well as social and economic development and regional stability. Cautious and intelligent policies for supporting nation-building processes do, therefore, serve a purpose. However, we should guard against thinking of the concept as a simple solution that can be applied everywhere regardless of local conditions. The risks and resources that need to be allocated are just too high (see Hippler, concluding chapter of this book).

Furthermore, it is not helpful to rid the nation-building concept of its essence and use it merely as a collective category for all non-military political instruments or as a synonym for peace-keeping, which is what frequently happens. The process of integration or fragmentation of societies and states is too important a matter in foreign, development and peace policy terms for it to be lost sight of through schematic usages of the term. As presently used, 'nation-building' can be a euphemism for imperial control, an empty entreaty formula to conceal one's own helplessness or a key concept of development policy and crisis prevention. In the latter case, it is however necessary to give the term meaning, be aware of its limitations and traps, sound out its chances and shape it into a concept that can be applied. It is for these purposes that the contributors to this book would like to throw light on a number of background factors and outline associated problems and suggestions. This first part focuses on important general conditions and issues, while the second part looks at current case examples of nation-building. The third and final part discusses questions of possible political approaches.

NOTE

1. Re the significance and change of political identities, see Hippler (2001).

REFERENCES

Atwood, J. Brian (1994) 'Nation Building and Crisis Prevention in the Post-Cold War World', *Brown Journal of World Affairs*, Vol. 2, No. 1, pp. 11–17.

Eriksen, Thomas Hylland (1993) 'A Future-Oriented, Non-Ethnic Nationalism? – Mauritius as an Exemplary Case', *Ethnos*, Vol. 58, pp. 197–221.

FAZ (Frankfurter Allgemeine Zeitung) (1994) 'Mit und bald ohne Aristide taumelt Haiti wieder ins Ungewisse', *FAZ*, 16 December 1994, p. 8.

Greenfeld, Liah (1992) *Nationalism: Five Roads to Modernity* (Cambridge).

Haig, Alexander M. (1994) 'Nation Building: A Flawed Approach', *Brown Journal of World Affairs*, Vol. 2, No. 1 (Winter), pp. 7–10.

Hippler, Jochen (2001) 'Kultur und Wissen: Trends und Interdependenzen', in Development and Peace Foundation, *Globale Trends 2002 – Fakten, Analysen, Prognosen*, ed. by Ingomar Hauchler, Dirk Messner and Franz Nuscheler (Frankfurt/M.), pp. 135–55.

Hippler, Jochen (2002) *Ethnicity, State, and Nation-Building – Experiences, Policies and Conceptualization*, Manuscript: <www.jochen-hippler.de/Aufsatze/Nation-Building/nation-building.html>.

Lenhart, Lioba (1992) 'Indonesien: Die Konzeption einer nationalen Kultur im Kontext des nation building', *Orientierungen – Zeitschrift zur Kultur Asiens*, special edition on Indonesia, pp. 83–103.

Lipset, Seymour Martin (1963) *The First New Nation: The United States in Historical and Comparative Perspective* (London).

Newsweek (1994) 'Can Haiti be Saved? – Nation-Building: Clinton is Avoiding the Term, but That's the Job He's In', *Newsweek*, 3 October 1994, pp. 16ff.

Rivkin, Arnold (1969) *Nation-Building in Africa: Problems and Prospects* (New Brunswick).

UN Chronicle (1994) published by the United Nations Organization (New York, June).

2
Globalisation and Nation-building – Not a Contradiction in Terms

Rainer Tetzlaff

Globalisation and nationalism by no means have to be perceived as distinct opposites or harmonious partners per se. They appear, rather, as two unequal forces in a global match of interests and identities which, however, have to be precariously balanced through political endeavours. It has always been the exclusive mandate of the nation-state to set frontiers, defend borders and property and increase the individual's possibilities of self-development for the good of society; and there are no indications that it will cease to be able to exercise this responsibility – though it must adapt to do so. This chapter therefore supports the thesis that all the current popular talk of the alleged end of the nation-state in the non-European world has little foundation and that the disappearance of the national Leviathan would also not be desirable (Tetzlaff 2001).

What has changed, however, is the claim to exclusivity: the state can now only perform its core functions in coordination with other decision-makers, together forming a *transnational multilevel system* made up of local, national and global players of state and non-state provenance (Zürn 1998; Wagner 2001).

What the reaction of national governments or social movements is to the representatives and influences of globalisation – aggressive rejection or a more receptive and expectant attitude – will likely depend on the specific development opportunities and prospects for the society concerned. There are already considerable differences in the national discourses conducted by the elites in the domains of power, education and the economy in the diverse global and cultural regions regarding their views on what is perceived as the challenge of globalisation (Tetzlaff 2000). What some see as a welcome opportunity to assert themselves in terms of international competition (for example China and South Korea), others find to be a threat to their own institutions and interests which has to be averted (Hindu nationalism in India or Sharia apologists in Muslim-Arab states).

Governments and state classes have an important function with regard to the winners and losers in the globalisation process, even if only in political-ideological terms in some cases. The regulative idea of national sovereignty assumes a greater role for postcolonial societies in which the trauma of colonisation and outside domination still exists than for the countries of the European Union, for example, whose national sovereignty has been extended in part to pan-European levels, thereby making it virtually multilateral.

GLOBALISATION AND THE CONTRADICTORY TWOFOLD NATURE OF THE INTERNATIONAL SYSTEM AFTER 1989

At first sight, globalisation and nationalism could appear to be a logical contradiction: if globalisation, as generally assumed, is an expression for the removal of national borders (denationalisation) and the transnational integration of exchange relations, the emergence or maintaining of sovereign nation-states with fixed borders and their own identity must then appear anachronistic and 'inappropriate'. Accordingly, the continued existence of nation-states would be poorly suited to a transnational global society in which transcontinental and transcultural migration is very much on the increase, which is proud of its common international institutions (such as the International Criminal Court) and which insists on universally valid values like democracy, the rule of law and human rights. Would it not be possible in the future for supranational state structures or transnationally networked societies to completely or partially replace the classic nation-state in the world outside Europe? Is the Israeli military historian, Martin van Creveld (1999), perhaps on the right track with his theory of the impending 'demise' of the nation-state that has evolved over centuries – as a consequence of the internationalisation of technology and the excessive demands placed on the national welfare state?

On closer consideration, it quickly becomes evident that such a linear notion of the development of a global society and its nation-state elements towards increasing political homogenisation ending in the forming of one global culture encompassing all nations is false (Hippler 2001; Wagner 2001). It is not linear progress towards a specifiable goal (for example a global state) that characterises the reality of international relations but, much more so, the *simultaneity of contradictory courses* in regionally and culturally different arenas of world politics which have shown amazing persistence. The systemic international competitiveness of national production and accumulation 'sites' with an innovative local culture is the central idea of economic neoliberalism.

There are, naturally enough, winners and losers in a worldwide market system with its omnipresent global players such as transnational companies and banks. While the fast-developing Asian countries, for example, have displayed a positive *developmental nationalism*, in states cut off from the substantial profit possibilities of the global market – those excluded economically from the global society – a more aggressive nationalism against the 'unjust' international world around them can be expected. Arab nationalism since the founding of the state of Israel can be cited as a prominent example in this respect (Kepel 2002).

The attitude towards globalisation differs greatly in regional and social terms due to the fact that, besides the (desired) acceleration and intensification of all types of exchange relationships, globalisation also brings about an (unintended but accepted) polarisation into rich and poor, which stirs up *national aversions to outside influences* and competitors. Breaches perceived as 'injustices' can be seen and experienced more today in a globalised public domain than was previously the case. Cooperation between national economies, states and societies, global players and locally established players has led only very partially to more growth and freedom for those involved, frequently causing, on the contrary, increasing social inequality and injustice – which provokes emotional reactions among groups of losers. 'Political antidotes' (Beck 1997) are therefore needed.

The number, duration and ferocity of 'new wars' and ethnic conflicts in Africa and Asia indicate that there is – in the political sense – no such thing as a global village because villages generally have public order structures, market policing, a local judge and civil self-control mechanisms. The international system in its globalised form is only beginning to become acquainted with mechanisms for governing beyond what have been classic nation-states for the last 200 years – for example transnational regimes.

The road to an institutionalised rational *global domestic policy* – and it is towards this utopia of a non-violent world with civil coexistence of heterogeneous peoples and cultures on the basis of humanitarian intervention and just reconciliation of interests that we should be orientating ourselves – is still a long one. To be successful, it also needs, above all, national agents to prepare the necessary change and structure it in a socially acceptable manner, thus legitimising it to the domestic public.

This theory of the indispensability of the national factor can be substantiated by the *contradictory twofold nature of the international system*. There is already such a close transnational interrelation in the economic, ecological and scientific-technical respect that we can rightly speak of a structurally interdependent global economy, a global risk society (Beck 1997) or a globalised modern age. The 'One World' at the beginning of the twenty-first century is thus becoming increasingly interlinked through global players from the economic and scientific domains, which social scientists refer to as 'structural interdependence'; at the same time, however, globalisation is, in the form of rapid socioeconomic change, also giving rise to uprooting at an individual level as a result of the fragmentation and dissolution of evolved orders.

This being torn out of one's roots forces the individual to search for inner security, which they can find in the cultural-religious or ethnic-national milieu. These are the two main forms in which identity can nowadays be found (or invented) as a reaction to globalisation.

POLITICISATION OF CULTURAL DIFFERENCES IN THE SEARCH FOR NATIONAL SECURITY

In many supposedly 'postmodern', 'postcolonial' societies, ethnic awareness, conceptions of the world influenced by ethnic-religious factors and ethnically determined action by individuals, parties, groups and movements are a political fact that is to be expected, especially in view of distribution conflicts and crisis situations. They have an increasing need to be sure of themselves and have a secured identity, which is often to be achieved by disassociation from potential or real rivals. The search for a culturally defined identity becomes important and elemental in such times.

Generally, such manifestations of political culture act as a social control mechanism. Ethnicity – first instrumentalised by the European colonial rulers for purposes of power – still performs orientational functions in African societies, in particular. On the one hand, it promises individuals and self-defined 'we' groups emotional support and cognitive orientation, while it can, on the other hand – as a player acting collectively – release huge potential for violence, as shown by the genocide in Rwanda in 1994, for example.

This was not a spontaneous outburst of collective rage or ethnic feelings of hatred but, rather, the calculation of a modern elite encompassing all occupational groups which saw the preservation of its power jeopardised by the growing ethnopolitical opposition – including the threat posed by an ethnic minority of exiles in neighbouring Uganda (the Tutsis). In this existential borderline situation, it decided on the extreme – the mass murder of brothers, cousins and neighbours, who were at the same time economic and political rivals – with the strategy of a collective crime involving as many players as possible pursued as a perverted act of nation-building. What is disturbing is that the politically constructed national entity, which lays claim to a state of its own, can again and again, as a constructed cultural identity, develop such monstrous importance for resolving non-ethnic conflicts that cultural differences are instrumentalised as a 'political weapon' by partners in dialogue.

We should bear in mind that ethnically defined identity in 'postcolonial' situations may not be underestimated or played down as an anachronistic relic of the uncivilised premodern age that will die out in the end but, rather, something to be regarded as an artificial, non-contingent concomitant in societies torn out of their foundations by the turbulences of globalisation. The weaker the traditional nation-state becomes, the greater the chances are of politicised ethnicity partially taking its place. A development of this kind towards ethnic segmentation would, in the light of all the experience gathered so far, proceed in an extremely violent manner 'since citizenship and ethnicity are two contradictory principles of democratic political legitimacy' (Castells 2003:113).

The *politicisation of cultural differences* by rival groups is a popular phenomenon nowadays in almost all regions of the world, in both rich and poor countries, even if the causes are different. The politicisation of ethnicity or ethnonationalism is only one variant of the politicisation of cultural differences; another lies in the politicisation of religious creeds, which can eventually culminate in fundamentalism. What the two have in common is the difference between content and form. The instrumentalisation of cultural difference stems in most cases from the temptation of power-conscious leaders to justify differences of position in the struggle for material advantages or for defending 'inherited privileges' or to assert material claims against 'others' – that is those less entitled and less worthy from the viewpoint of the perpetrators.

VARIANTS OF NATIONALISM THAT ACTUALLY EXIST IN THE NON-EUROPEAN WORLD AS REACTIONS TO OUTSIDE RULE AND GLOBALISATION

Resistance to colonial outside rule was – seen in historical terms – the context for the emergence of nationalism in the Third World, beginning with charismatic leaders like Mahatma Gandhi in India and Sun Yat-sen in China. Invoking the ideal of the French Revolution and the right of national self-determination proclaimed by US President Woodrow Wilson back in World War I as a regulatory concept for a peaceful world of sovereign states, this anti-imperialistic liberational nationalism also displayed its effect in those places where nations did not even exist as yet in the sense of a community of common origin or a politically organised community with a common will (following European models). National movements led by intellectuals with experience of the West sufficed to ignite the idea of freedom and self-determination even among an ethnically fragmented colonial population. As the foundations were often missing – that is the transformation of ethnocultural communities, via a common internal market, into societies based on shared interests and solidarity facilitated by the state – the nation-states becoming sovereign nations mostly remained rather weak structures. Only good leadership – as in Singapore, Taiwan and South Korea, for example – was able to transform fictive assertions into reality (Schubert 2000; Castells 2003:267ff.).

Postcolonial nationalism still exists today, appearing in at least two functional variations as economically inspired developmental nationalism and as defensive nationalism fed by cultural-religious factors. In frequent cases, the two have also served to strengthen each other. Communist China – the biggest nation on Earth – has so far been the most convincing example of this and, at the same time, the one with historically the most powerful effect. Gunter Schubert pointed out that, in post-Maoist China, both the culturally traditionalist intellectuals and the enlightened, democratic representatives of the educated elite in modern Chinese nationalism

> saw an answer from China to the challenge of the West and unavoidable national conflicts of interest in the course of globalisation. Nationalism was to close the ranks of the Chinese behind their state as the champion of the nation's fundamental interests. The legitimation of state rule and state action was, as a rule, confined to a successful modernisation policy, which required a *strong* state. (Schubert 2002:253; emphasis in the original)

One would hardly be mistaken in assuming that this state-based *developmental nationalism* was and is regarded as a model by numerous elitist groups of other Third World countries. However, only a small number of countries have had the chance of translating this ideal of the nationally strong developing state into reality. Developmental nationalism signifies the strategy of a patriotic state class and power elite to stimulate, consolidate and symbolically legitimise social hopes and endeavours for a better life for the population in competition with other populations. It is the special relationship between the active state and a population which can be mobilised that has made the great achievements of the developing state in Asia possible.

In its second variation, nationalism appears in the form of mostly substate, partial *defensive nationalism* – as a defensive reaction to disappointed hopes of modernisation, as a protest against economic exclusion and/or cultural 'swamping'. It is often associated with a desperate search for a new cultural identity or reestablishment of one's own cultural values and notions of order, with the possibility of hatred playing a constituent role between ethnic groups – especially in India and sub-Saharan Africa. In India, for example, a partly xenophobic, aggressive Hindu nationalism has emerged in the course of globalisation which has come out against the visible symbols of globalisation – against multinational companies like Coca-Cola and Kentucky Fried Chicken.

The most significant reaction worldwide to the ambivalent challenges of globalisation, starting with European colonialism and continuing with the Soviet occupation of Afghanistan, is taking place in the *area of Islamic culture*. The only major countermovement against the globalisation of Western origin has emerged there – an international 'cultural struggle' of major significance in world history from the viewpoint of many Islamists since 1991.

In the Muslim world, a religiously inspired Islamic fundamentalism developed after 1967 from the ruins of Nasser-style (socialist) Arab nationalism which turned away from the classic nationalism of the individual (Arab) states and attempted to build a new *non-national identity* in the Islamic faith – with little prospect of lasting success, in the view of the French researcher of Islam, Gilles Kepel (though prior to September 11, 2001). In his book entitled *The Black Book of the Jihad* – a crusade by the losers of modernisation conducted against the presumptuous culture of the West – he interprets the fascination of Islamism as follows:

> The ambiguity of its message, in which both the bearded capitalist and the person living in the slums can find themselves, makes it easier to spread ... By promising to restore the just society from the primeval times of Islam – the state established by the Prophet in Medina – Islamism embodies a utopia which holds all the more attraction as it opposes regimes that have gone downhill prematurely through corruption, economic and moral decline, claim to absolute authority and suppression of basic civil rights – the norm at that time in the Islamic world. (Kepel 2002:29)

The projection of the unique Islamic religious community still gains its strength today from the awareness – no doubt further nourished by the second Iraq war – that, as a Muslim, one is surrounded by a hostile world.

This overview of the manifestations and historical contexts for the emergence of nationalism in the non-European world may suffice to reinforce the belief that neither the nation-state nor nationalism has been doomed to demise everywhere in the world. Although it may be that 'the majority of new states in Asia and Africa present a pitiful sight' (Crefeld 1999:365), both the successes and misfortunes of the postcolonial developing state (up to and including breakdown of the state) have made us aware of the political significance of national emotions and yearnings. This theory is also supported by the long-continued existence of a number of political parties in Africa which see themselves as a symbol of the nation (for example the TANU in Tanzania).

SECOND WAVE OF NATIONAL LIBERATION AND THE DILEMMA OF DEPENDENCE: EXTERNAL SOVEREIGNTY ANNUITIES RATHER THAN NATIONAL FISCAL CAPACITIES

In conclusion – following the thesis of the national reaction to external stimuli – an issue needs to be addressed which often poses a major dilemma for the elites in countries encumbered with high debt levels: the compulsion to adopt structural adjustment policies imposed by creditors in order to retain creditworthiness at international level. Where such compulsion to adapt to international power structures goes beyond the limit of what can reasonably be expected nationally, resistance can be anticipated which may take on national forms. There are not only 'postnational' constellations in the globalised world, as Jürgen Habermas (1998) contended with regard to Europe. We may even have to reckon with a *second wave of national liberation* here and there. Whereas the first wave of national liberation movements was directed against colonial foreign rule by the whites and subsequently towards the realisation of national development utopias, today's national protest by established governments is opposed to two manifestations of global players: to 'foreign infiltration' by the 'white devils' in the form of global business enterprises and their political backers as well as the politically insensitive conditions imposed for the granting of loans by the Bretton Woods twins, the World Bank and the International Monetary Fund (IMF).

It is the latter, in particular, that have caused uproar in very recent times. The partly concealed, partly publicly stage-managed national struggle by government elites against a structural adjustment policy that is perceived as socially unjust or excessively severe and the pursuance of which is demanded of indebted Third World governments by the World Bank and the IMF has become a principal area of conflict in North–South relations. Where economy and reform measures called for from outside are perceived as national humiliation in the developing or transitional country (which are often objectively logical in essence), broad solidarity among the political public against the external trouble-makers, the 'neocolonialists', can be expected. National honour is supposedly at stake.

On the other hand, the political class in numerous poorer developing countries in Asia and especially Africa is dependent to a very great extent on so-called *sovereignty annuities* – that is donations from abroad mostly in the context of international development cooperation, which gives rise to a dilemma regarding what action should be taken.

The single fact of belonging to the government and being able to represent the state recognised under international law vis-à-vis the outside world – regardless of how state power was gained and is maintained – gives the political class greater leeway for action to pursue selfish goals. We are therefore confronted in numerous cases with a 'national' *sovereignty of the elite* supported from outside – in contrast to a democratically representative form of government founded on sovereignty of the people.

Any reduction of such annuity payments threatened or actually enforced as a result of a disagreement with the Bretton Woods twins can have a politically destabilising effect. In extreme cases, it can even lead to the collapse of the state – as occurred in the early 1990s in Somalia, Liberia and Sierra Leone. If the state budget to be distributed becomes so small that only sections of the ruling elite coalition can obtain sinecure and position, there is a threat that the 'bonding' which served to integrate the society up to that point in time will crumble, with the result that the national political class will disintegrate into a narrow ethnonationalistic section rallying around the state president and his security apparatus with the remainder bitterly defending the state's power, while also fragmenting into several subnational (ethnic) rebel formations. After the breakdown of the state's monopoly of force, there will be ethnic militias and other forms of privatised force fighting on both sides. Where these want to capture state power for themselves in order to be in receipt of and enjoy the state's sovereignty annuities or are satisfied with occupying a diamond or gold mine producing foreign exchange revenues – the national project of the first decades of independence will have failed. Bringing it back to real life with broadly established expectations of a better common future is difficult but not impossible, as in the example of previously successful Mozambique, which is, with external assistance, recovering from one of Africa's civil wars involving the heaviest casualties and now growing together again. Global players act here as indispensable catalysts and sponsors of second-phase nation-building.

The prototype of *protesting nationalism* against unreasonable international demands is portrayed by the President of Malaysia, Mahathir bin Mohamad. During the Asian crisis, he defied the 'recommendations' of the Bretton Woods institutions, which would have logically resulted in further impoverishment of the middle classes. Despite the objections coming from Washington, he imposed a ban on the export of foreign exchange and stabilised the economy in a comparatively successful manner by means of foreign exchange management and foreign trade control. This prestigious success – which attracted much attention in the specialist literature (Schubert 2000) – often accompanied by anti-imperialistic rhetoric in Asia, underlines the importance of governments' ability to take action at national level, especially in times of crisis, to intervene in the socially blind market economy for the benefit of one's own national interests.

CONCLUSION: TAKING AWAY THE UNDERLYING POVERTY AND DESPAIR FROM THE FURIES OF NATIONALISM

Although economic globalisation (in the form of the neoliberal market and borrowing systems) can, with its opportunities for action and existential risks, undermine governments' options for political control (especially in relation to foreign trade policy), it does not displace nationalism as a historically effective social force.

The substantial ongoing successes in the development of Taiwan and South Korea, Singapore and the People's Republic of China cannot be understood without a profound developmental nationalism (with or without the stimulant of belief in 'Asian values'). In these cases, globalisation – that is the politically desired opening-up of world markets for manufactured Asian products and processed agricultural goods from selected (pro-Western) countries – has accelerated the process of economic growth and modernisation steered by the nation-state. Japan has played a role as a model in this regard, while elitist political vanguard parties with universally propagated emblems of national sovereignty have been (and are) the vehicle by which excessive propagandist developmental nationalism is cultivated.

What is more astonishing is the fact that the national will for self-assertion does not come to a standstill in the case of economic failures or even the breakdown of the state. The most recent development on the former state territory of Zaire (now known again as Congo), whose raw materials have been fought over by the 'sovereign' neighbouring states of Uganda, Rwanda and Zimbabwe, has led to an amazing will for self-assertion on the part of the Congolese in a number of regions with high proportions of foreigners (soldiers from Rwanda and Uganda). However, there have also been conflicting processes in very recent times with transnational alliances emerging in order to be able to survive under conditions of war. Nevertheless, this huge land, which is only weakly integrated, has so far not fallen apart entirely and the endeavours for national reunification of the government and regional rebel groups are continuing despite great difficulties. The prospect of collecting sovereignty and development aid annuities from abroad may be playing a decisive role, though this presupposes the restoration of statism. The players involved will, in this respect, weigh up the anticipated annuity revenues against the advantages they gain from legal and illegal exports of raw materials from war zones.

To summarise, it can be said that, in a world with a substantial and growing *disparity of power* between states and developing regions as a result of economic globalisation, national governments are losing some of the classic type of economic sovereignty (gauged against their ability to decide autonomously on budget expenditure and productive investment, as the first postcolonial generation of leaders was still able to do). Depending on the imperatives of globalisation, however, new opportunities are also emerging with increasing wealth for shaping the state in a way that can serve national ambition as a seedbed. There are at least *three core areas* that remain the preserve of the national state and which justify and legitimise its rule both internally and externally. These are:

- maintaining the state's monopoly of force and a state under the rule of law; this is and remains the only interlocutor regarding the protection of human rights;
- securing international competitiveness of the national location through infrastructure and education policy measures (transport systems; human capital) and defensive reactions against undesirable global market effects;
- reintegration of the weaker members of society and potential losers of globalisation, the 'new poor', into national or regional, formal or informal economic cycles. The nation-state is and remains the arena for the struggle to achieve greater social justice, especially in the face of transnational irritations.

The real problem – as already indicated – can be expected on the part of those losing out to globalisation. It is therefore to be anticipated that governments will play the 'national card' and employ steered nationalistic emotions as a political resource where they themselves, for reasons of holding onto power or because of sheer despair over ruined development opportunities, see no way out other than to let loose the furies of nationalism against supposed rivals in order to realise their own objectives.

REFERENCES

Beck, Ulrich (1997) *Was ist Globalisierung?* (Frankfurt/M.).

Castells, Manuel (2003) *Das Informationszeitalter: Wirtschaft, Gesellschaft, Kultur, Vol. III: Jahrtausendwende* (Opladen).

Creveld, Martin van (1999) *Aufstieg und Untergang des Staates* (Munich).

Habermas, Jürgen (1998) *Die postnationale Konstellation. Politische Essays* (Frankfurt/M.).

Hippler, Jochen (2001) 'Kultur und Wissen: Trends und Interdependenzen', in Development and Peace Foundation, *Globale Trends 2002 – Fakten, Analysen, Prognosen*, ed. by Ingomar Hauchler, Dirk Messner and Franz Nuscheler (Frankfurt/M.), pp. 135–55.

Kepel, Gilles (2002) *Das Schwarzbuch des Dschihad. Aufstieg und Niedergang des Islamismus* (Munich/Zurich).

Schubert, Gunter (2000) 'Die Asienkrise als Grenzmarkierung der Globalisierung? Bewertungen aus der Region', in Rainer Tetzlaff (ed.), *Weltkulturen unter Globalisierungsdruck. Erfahrungen und Antworten aus den Kontinenten* (ONE World series of the Development and Peace Foundation No. 9, Bonn), pp. 120–50.

Schubert, Gunter (2002) *Chinas Kampf um die Nation. Dimensionen nationalistischen Denkens in der VR China, Taiwan und Hongkong an der Jahrtausendwende* (IFA, Hamburg).

Tetzlaff, Rainer (ed.) (2000) *Weltkulturen unter Globalisierungsdruck. Erfahrungen und Antworten aus den Kontinenten* (ONE World series of the Development and Peace Foundation No. 9, Bonn).

Tetzlaff, Rainer (2001) 'Ist der fragmentierte Staat in Afrika entbehrlich? Fragmentierte Gesellschaften zwischen Staatszerfall und sozialer Anomie, Kriegsherrentum und privater Organisation von Überlebenssicherheit', in L. Marfaing and B. Reinwald (eds), *Afrikanische Beziehungen* (Hamburg/Berlin/London), pp. 201–28.

Wagner, Bernd (ed.) (2001) *Kulturelle Globalisierung. Zwischen Weltkultur und kultureller Fragmentierung* (series of publications by the Hessian Society for Democracy and Ecology 13, Essen).

Zürn, Michael (1998) *Regieren jenseits des Nationalstaates. Globalisierung und Denationalisierung als Chance* (Frankfurt/M.).

3

Democratisation and Nation-building in 'Divided Societies'

Joanna Pfaff-Czarnecka[1]

In the mid 1970s, two processes of global scope began virtually simultaneously. Numerous countries in Africa, Latin America, Asia and Europe were caught in the maelstrom of far-reaching political reforms of the 'third wave of democratisation' (Huntington 1991). In aspiring to nation-building, many governments adopted democratic institutional designs through constitutional reforms. At the same time, growing civil society movements were giving expression to the global recognition of democratic values. Since then, working towards democratic reforms not only has a high degree of legitimacy in the West; the expectations placed in such reforms are high.

The challenges faced by a large number of countries since that time include a second global phenomenon, referred to in general and simplified terms as 'ethnic conflict'. Whether ethnic conflicts have only escalated since the 1970s and what is understood by them is the subject of heated debates. Whatever the case, they attract worldwide attention in the media, political think-tanks and scientific research. Ethnicity has become a successful mobilisation formula and a permanent element of political communication. It would appear that today's ethnic leaders can fall back on global experiences with regard to how ethnic mobilisation should be organised and political discourse conducted so as to gain public attention and political ground as well as have themselves invited to negotiations by governments.

In numerous countries (postsocialist states, Latin America, Southern Asia), it is becoming apparent that ethnic categories are recognised, at least in part, as a mode of social integration and ethnic demands acknowledged as a matter of concern to minorities in the course of nation-building processes. This normally necessitates far-reaching institutional reforms and a new conceptualisation of the respective 'nation'. Ethnic leaders or representatives of minorities are becoming increasingly involved in the preparation of new constitutions. Many of the constitutions adopted in the 1990s now also recognise the ethnic diversity within the state's borders in addition to universal franchise, separation of powers and freedom of information and assembly. The reforms are intended to overcome ethnic conflicts and permanently secure peaceful coexistence between ethnic groups.

However, ethnic conflicts can easily erupt in phases of radical democratic change in particular. The democratic promise of equal opportunities can encourage the ethnicisation of politics (Wimmer 2002), provoke vehement power struggles for state resources (Hippler, Chapter 1, this volume; Wimmer 2002) and give rise to the ethnicisation of political communication (Pfaff-Czarnecka 2001). The supporters of democratic mobilisation are ethnically and/or according to religious allegiance of heterogeneous composition in many places, and their expectations are growing rapidly. The emergence of democracy is seen by many as a favourable opportunity to convey demands; the feeling of unjustness is intensifying. Therefore, although democratic reforms can – as will be shown – contribute towards abating conflicts, they can also cause them to escalate.

THREE MODELS OF NATIONAL UNITY

While currently in the debates surrounding national unity many scholars' attention lies on the potentially centrifugal nature of minority demands, a number of authors stress that a differentiated mode of integrating minorities was already inherent in earlier attempts at nation-building. Indeed, many countries have gone through three stages in the course of nation-building, that is from (1) ethnically complex and hierarchically organised state societies to (2) nations negating their cultural diversity to (3) today's pluralistic-egalitarian models, which now conceptualise national unity that would nevertheless recognise diversity.

A brief examination of these three models can be useful in assessing the new democratic designs for two reasons: it enables an insight into the dynamics of the formation of 'we-groups' (Elwert 1997) and, in particular, the mutually dependent processes of nationalist and ethnic closure. It will also be shown that many of the minority demands expressed nowadays can be seen as a response to previous institutional arrangements and are often reactions to past national structures which have caused ethnic conflicts to flare up. The decisive character of the democratic forms of organisation applied in the third model for transforming ethnic conflicts is expressed against the background of the two previous models.

First model: imperium

The first model sees national unity as an imperium (Gellner 1983). This type of predemocratic or rudimentarily democratic states comprised a religiously and culturally distinct population within the country's borders with partially semi-autonomous administrative units and, frequently, a hierarchic order. The class orders, colonial or caste hierarchies, provided for superordination and subordination, segregation and a more or less pronounced division of labour. The legal systems differentiated between groups and ranks. A low hierarchic status restricted the rights of the collective and excluded its members from deriving benefits. The continuity of customs, languages and religions of the sections of the population was, however, hardly affected.

Whoever ruled, it was their religion that dominated in many places. Once the religious-cultural framework had been defined, the rulers were in no way concerned with persuading the population to adopt their culture or convert to their faith. There was no desire to create a unified culture or encourage communication among one's subjects (Gellner 1983). It was indeed useful to emphasise differences in order to set oneself apart from the lower ranks.

It is a known fact that such principles of hierarchic order imply two possibilities. The boundaries between individual groups can – as in the racism of National Socialism in 1930s and 1940s Germany, the apartheid system of South Africa or the racial segregation of North America – be completely sealed off in order to prevent intermixing or 'contagion'. On the other hand, hierarchic orders of this type provide ample scope for distance, religious-cultural autonomy and – contradictory as this may sound – mutual convergence. This model made room for 'integration through difference' maintained by hierarchic means.

Second model: culturally homogeneous nation of the modern age

Paradoxically, the implementation of the second, assimilatory model, which conceived nations as culturally homogeneous entities, divided the populations in many countries. This political form, shaped by Western modernity and dominant in a large number of developing countries in the postcolonial phase was based – though often merely in terms of rhetoric – on the modern principles of democracy, citizenship, sovereignty of the people, rationally organised administration and politics, equality of all individuals before the law, and guarantees of status in the welfare state system.

In many countries, the doctrine of neutrality of the state in relation to religion and culture was interpreted in such a way that cultural and religious forms of expression were kept away from the public domain, though this did not apply to the national culture, to which great importance was attached as a defining characteristic. The modernisation endeavours in numerous countries 'of the South' combined the idea of social progress with redefining the key notions seen as constituting national unity. The state elites were preoccupied with the question how the national culture could be shaped to serve progress. The discourse on modernisation was understood by many as a catchup development, also in the sense of steered cultural change. Related to developing countries, it served to focus attention on the nation-building processes underpinned by regulated norms (cf. Hippler, Chapter 1, this volume). Communication among society as a whole was encouraged so as to develop a national force and strength united in striving for progress.

In most places, the culture of the national elites was declared the binding culture, while minority cultures and religions deemed to be backward or even dissident were actively discouraged. The protagonists of modernisation even predicted that cultural barriers would disappear anyway with the development of productive forces. If the maintaining of minority cultures was permitted at all, they were confined to the private sphere. There was no place for minority symbols in national representations, with official rhetoric even occasionally denouncing them as damaging. Minority languages were systematically ignored, 'backward' religious practices derided and the contribution of minorities to the nation's history negated.

The thesis forwarded in ethnicity research that ethnicisation processes can in no way be regarded as retrogressive dynamics steeped in tradition undermining the modern age has been illustrated by many examples (Anderson 1996). They should be seen more as the result of the ethnicisation beginning in the first phase of European nation-building when national entities were thought of as quasi-ethnic identities. Subsequently, the mode of nationalistic integration was professed to be a 'modern' script for ethnic mobilisation. Wimmer (2002) goes even further by contending that, in particular, modern welfare-state status guarantees became a factor for excluding those persons and groups not regarded as true members of the nation. It was thus precisely in the process of democratic development that the drawbacks of modern nation-building made themselves felt.

Third model: pluricultural[2] integration

Exclusion from public representative bodies, pejorative portrayals of minority cultures, plus obstacles to participating in politics and administration for members of minorities lacking the necessary cultural, social or economic capital was, in many countries, turned into a negative integration matrix against which increasing resistance started to build up. The ethnicisation of politics, in the course of attempts to democratise, varied in degree and intensity from country to country.

Discrimination against and oppression of minorities were multifarious in the past, and the matters of concern raised by themselves and their advocates today are correspondingly numerous. It is, in the first instance, a question of official representations and, in particular, a matter of enhancing the presence of one's own culture in the public sphere. There is also a struggle for recognition of rights to cultural and religious freedom, which concern both the public (establishment of buildings of worship) and private (family law) spheres. Secondly, political representation is demanded and with it the lowering of barriers preventing members of minorities from participating in public administration. Thirdly, it is a matter of the (re)distribution of economic resources and opportunities of access to public institutions, such as schools. Regions that are, in the main, ethnically homogeneous demand greater competences in disposing of locally produced resources.

The constitutions adopted in many countries in the course of the third wave of democratisation established the 'multiethnic' and 'multilingual' character of national societies, thus taking account of cultural and religious diversity. In other countries, members of minorities and other marginalised groups are making ever more frequent demands for constitutional recognition of their specific matters of concern.

'DIVIDED SOCIETIES', NATION-BUILDING AND DEMOCRATIC MODELS

Ethnic conflicts can prove real tests for countries in which democratic reforms are just getting going. Demands put forward by ethnic leaders put a strain on what are often fragile nation-building processes. It is extensively recognised, at the same time, that the building of democracy cannot be achieved without making provisions to transform ethnic conflicts and safeguard peaceful coexistence between majorities and minorities. How effective the different models are is, however, disputed.

Reynolds (2002) speaks of a partially new 'architecture' of democracy consisting of both political and administrative institutions established to overcome conflict and facilitate peaceful coexistence. Some of these designs, which have since been adopted de jure in many countries and implemented with greater or lesser success, represent important reforms of previous legal and political institutions. The fact that they normally counteract centralist and/or assimilatory tendencies produces more scope for ethnically differentiated and institutional solutions adapted to specific interests. In turning away from the individualistic-universalistic body of thought of liberalism, collective categories are once again playing an important role.

A minority of scholars embrace the view that developing democratic designs is without consequence for the creation of peaceful existence in 'divided societies'. Interdisciplinary research dominated by political science proceeds to an ever-increasing extent from the standpoint that political institutions influence the logic and effectiveness of democratic politics. Economic upturn alone does not provide an adequate basis for democratisation. Guarantees of status would be required additionally for weak members of society, also under tough economic conditions. If these were not granted nowadays, it would have delegitimising effects for the given governments as well as the international players involved.

In the following, we will concentrate on the most important democratic innovations for transforming conflicts and securing peace in 'divided societies' – *concordance, local representation, federalism* and *cultural autonomy*.

Concordance

The concordance model allows the representatives of all important groups to participate in the political decision-making process and especially in the executive (Lijphart 2002). Instead of the majority making the decisions, in this model the central issues are settled, where possible, by consensus and through compromises between the communities regarded as forming constituent parts of the state. The model can assume a considerable variety of institutional forms: a large coalition cabinet made up of ethnic parties (e.g. in the context of the Malaysian and South African parliamentary systems), a large coalition cabinet according to quotas (e.g. linguistic, as in Belgium), quotas corresponding to the percentage allocation of the population when filling ministerial positions (India), representation of the largest parties in the executive (e.g. the Swiss Bundesrat (Government) is made up of the four largest parties, with the cantons they belong to and, therefore, their language also taken into account when electing its members (ministers)), or determining the most important posts in the executive (president, prime minister, speaker of the house of representatives) according to ethnic and/or religious affiliation (as in Lebanon and Cyprus) (Lijphart 2002).

Lijphart (2002) sees the most important advantages of this model in the settling of ethnic differences through the forming of coalitions and commitment to cooperation between the elites. He stresses that concordance offers the only option for the minority parties prepared to form a coalition to take a place in the cabinet and remain in it.

In 'divided societies', the potential of the concordance approach is seen by the relevant literature to be greatest where there is no strong majority. In contrast, if an ethnic majority leader knows he has 60 per cent of the population behind him, his willingness to make political concessions to minority leaders has to be rated as low (Horowitz 2002). In this constellation he will prefer a majority system. Majorities and minorities naturally have different interests in joining together to form a coalition.

Local representation

In some 'divided societies' electoral systems are geared in such a way as to guarantee the broadest and most diverse representation of minorities possible in the political bodies. The models vary: one provides for minorities being represented by their 'own' representatives, ideally in proportion to the percentage of the minorities among the overall population. This can be done by 'tailoring' the electoral system accordingly or through special forms of representation. Another model is aimed at the political integration of minorities rather than direct representation.

Well-known examples of electoral systems organised according to ethnic criteria can be found in Cyprus, India and Fiji. Local representation has been introduced in several countries – especially on the territory of the former Yugoslavia, but also in China and

Samoa. Such systems differ, as in the case of concordance, by virtue of their 'national character'. In India, for example, there are electoral quota systems for the so-called 'scheduled castes' and 'scheduled tribes'. On the island of Cyprus, Great Britain introduced a system of local representation under which the 50-seat house of representatives was made up of 35 Greeks and 15 Turks each elected by the members of their 'own' groups. The legislative assembly in Bosnia-Herzegovina comprises equal numbers of locally elected representatives of the Croatians, Bosnians and Serbs (Ghai 2002).

The advantage of this arrangement is that the matters of concern and goals of even small minorities can be represented through the local procedures (though a 3–5 per cent quota normally has to be exceeded). In the run-up to elections, this system can offer an incentive for the leadership of ethnic groups to join together. In this way, minority elites fearing an unfavourable election result can display their willingness to compromise to smaller groups so as to form pools of votes (Lijphart 2002). In order to be able to win the votes of smaller groups, the larger groups must, however, show that they are receptive to the goals of their smaller counterparts, which can lead to conflict within their own ranks, causing them to break up into factions (Horowitz 2002). Minority representatives who join stronger parties can, on the other hand, adapt to such an extent that they no longer adequately represent the interests of their own communities.

The problems of this model are considerable, however. Firstly, quotas often lead to feelings of resentment, especially – though not exclusively – on the part of the minorities. Secondly, where parliamentary seats are distributed in line with local quotas, as in Bosnia-Herzegovina, the parties' policies are extensively dominated by narrowly defined ethnic interests, boosting the success of extremist parties (Ghai 2002). Thirdly, ethnic differences, especially local prejudices, can be accentuated during the election campaign. Furthermore, mobilising ethnic votes, which highlights particularistic objectives, can turn attention away from the interests of society as a whole. Too little heed is often paid to the common interests of weak members of minority groups while, fourthly, ethnic elites are presented with a vehicle for political advancement. Norris (2002) presents empirical evidence against the thesis according to which electoral systems based on proportional representation have generated more support for the political system among ethnic minorities.

Federalism

In the search for institutional designs aimed at transforming ethnic conflicts, federalist structures are regarded as the best institutional option. The ideal of federalism is for all regions to have equal power and authority, with their relationship with the central political apparatus following identical rules. Still, asymmetric federalist systems are frequently designed to overcome ethnic conflicts. Territorial autonomy is an asymmetrical form of federalism and represents a special case in which one region is favoured vis-à-vis others. The aim of territorial autonomy is to allow ethnic and other groups to themselves resolve those matters that are of particular interest to them, while the interests of society as a whole are managed at a higher level (Ghai 2002). A special variant of asymmetric structures are the reservations for indigenous groups in the US, Canada, Australia and Scandinavia.

The advantages of the federal model lie in democratic participation, the sharing of sovereignty, greater flexibility in the political decision-making process and implementation of such decisions, plus the decentralisation of power. From the multicultural perspective, there is more scope in federal states for the goals of minorities to be articulated and more potential for them to be realised. Minorities are also often said to feel more secure in such a system.

In the multiculturalistic variant of federalism, experts recommend that the country be divided up into small territorial units to enable the administrative boundaries to coincide with ethnic boundaries. In the case of heterogeneous territorial units, the need to make compromises at a lower administrative level can provide valuable experience for political socialisation, which encourages people's readiness to recognise the political system. In the course of progressive regionalisation, the federal units can also be integrated at suprastate level and still remain members of the state (Ghai 2002).

The danger of secession is considered to be one of the problems of federalism. Where ethnic, religious or linguistic boundaries coincide with federal administrative units, the granting of partial autonomy can give rise to demands for greater autonomy. Gurr (1993) asserts, however, that empirical findings have suggested a different conclusion, i.e. that regional autonomy provides an effective means of overcoming regional conflicts, with endeavours towards separatism tending to be aroused more if partial autonomy is not granted. As with the other models, territorial divisions carried out along ethnic lines can, however, exacerbate the drawing of ethnic borders. With ethnic intermixing, in contrast, there is a risk of other minorities being subordinated to the 'majority minority'.

Cultural autonomy

Cultural autonomy can be an element of territorial autonomy or be institutionalised on a non-territorial basis (also referred to as 'corporate autonomy'). In both cases it comprises – as in China and India, for instance – a range of special provisions that may even differ within the national context. Cultural autonomy is accomplished within the framework of local commissions and committees – where politics is organised locally – as well as in the form of protection afforded to the collective. In many – for example postsocialist – countries, cultural committees have been set up to look after the interests of the various groups. These committees have the authority to collect taxes from the members and also receive public funds in many instances. The most important objective of such organisations is to preserve and strengthen the identity of the respective minorities, which is why special attention is paid to nurturing language, religion and customs.

A central constituent of cultural autonomy is what languages are raised to the standing of official languages, what religions receive official status and what school curricula content is decided upon. Legal pluralism is considered an important element, especially in the area of civil law, which can be regulated under customary or religious law. The recognition of traditional legal codes in addition to the dominant legal system can constitute an important measure for strengthening the rights of minorities. All in all, this approach helps – according to its advocates – to satisfy the players involved by enabling them to organise their affairs themselves, which is seen as conducive to a stable democracy.

Rules and regulations that deny protection of their culture to those members who do not belong to a minority are the subject of controversial discussion. A well-known example of this can be found in Canada with the restrictions imposed vis-à-vis the English language in Quebec. Internal rules of exclusion are equally controversial, for example in the case of the Mennonites, who may disinherit children marrying outside the group. On the other hand, cultural autonomy is seldom conceptualised as being binding for all members of society. Conversely, systems whose laws are strongly oriented towards individualist-universalist models (Germany, Switzerland) grant special provisions for members of religious or cultural minorities (for example exemption from swimming classes for female Muslim pupils) (Barry 2000).

Cultural autonomy models are criticised because they can exacerbate differences. Traditionalist-autocratic structures that go hand in hand with cultural autonomy and which deny rights to internal minorities and women are seen as problematic, with the power of definition remaining with the traditional elites. The models of cultural autonomy (like concordance) are considered suitable, at best, for the phase of de-escalating ethnic conflicts (Horowitz 2002).

ASSESSMENT OF THE MODELS

Although most of the democratic forms of organisation presented here are not new, they have only recently been applied in a large number of nation-state contexts. In many places, the implementation phases are too short to enable adequate evaluation of their success. What is certain is that the national constellations vary, with the size of the country, its geographical location, the proportions between majorities and minorities, their regional distribution, the historical course of their coexistence and past forms of social integration possibly exerting a decisive influence. For this reason, it is impossible to present uniform recipes or best practices that could be reapplied to other national contexts. Where democratic designs have proved successful, as in Northern Ireland for instance, these combine different institutions and practices. Horowitz (2002) points out that in young democracies like Bulgaria, for example, new state constitutions tend to be very eclectic and inconsistent, resulting already for this very reason in a mix of institutions.

The institutional models discussed here are viewed by their supporters as ways of reducing the potential for conflict. As Lijphart (2002) stresses, strong cohesion of internal groups and the drawing of more distinct boundaries do not necessarily lead to an escalation of conflict. The designs outlined lay claim to counteracting cultural and religious discrimination. It can therefore be assessed as something positive that implementation of these designs gives rise to demands for the recognition of culturally differing forms of thought, speech, action and measures against exclusion, assimilation and disparagement.

In the processes of building modern states (cf. the second model), little scope was left for the shaping and public recognition of cultural and religious diversity. The 'tyranny of the majorities', which was underpinned ideologically by state neutrality in matters of culture, was expressed – among other things – in the majority culture dominating the minorities. If the assimilatory logics of modernisation are now rejected, this is based on the insight that the discriminatory practices with which minorities were confronted in this phase of nation-building fanned the flames of their readiness for conflict and are, furthermore, incompatible with democratic principles and guarantees of status in relation to human rights. Recognition of the *matters of concern* of minorities – although not necessarily of the *rights* of minorities – within the international community now offers minorities (or at least their elites) the possibility to upset the balance of power dominated by majorities.

Our examination shows at the same time that democratic reforms without any further ethnic mobilisation can even encourage secession or ethnic segregation. Although institutional reforms outlining group boundaries can be perfectly justified in democratic terms, they can, however, run counter to democratisation. It is therefore necessary to ask to what extent such reforms involve the risk of intensifying interethnic barriers. The list of questions to be resolved is long:

- Are mutual resentments stirred up (including minority complexes on the part of the majorities)?
- Are identities in flux reinforced; does this result in compulsion towards internal homogenisation?
- Are the elites favoured?
- Is political and cultural conservatism encouraged?
- Are the matters of concern of weak members of minorities marginalised by emphasising 'ethnic objectives'?
- Are individual rights restricted and is collective pressure to adapt increased?
- Are internal minorities oppressed, does a male bias emerge?
- Are particularistic goals emphasised while matters concerning society as a whole are pushed to the bottom of political agendas; is there a lack of incentives for solidarity among society as a whole?
- Is the development of an identity 'in itself' (formation of 'we-groups') among loosely integrated groups encouraged which shares ethnic characteristics (Norris 2002)?
- Do leaders of ethnic minorities strive for fragmentation of political and administrative entities?

In view of the weaknesses of models referred to, which accentuate group boundaries, and of the not inconsiderable potential for intra- and interethnic conflict, the role of these models in processes of democratisation has to be described as ambivalent. Democratic organisational models that institutionalise ethnic boundaries can perform important functions in democratisation processes. However, over the long term they can also undermine the dynamics of democratisation and interfere with the building of a nation-state.

Antidiscrimination, cultural recognition and incentives for making political compromises are important achievements of young democracies in the course of nation-building. Both the settlement of conflicts and securing a lasting peace require appropriate institutionalised mechanisms for resolving conflicts. It is questionable, however, whether mechanisms and models oriented according to ethnic criteria are the optimum path to take. It would be better, rather, to strive for the pluricultural integration of the late modern age, which does not favour ethnic categories in its guarantees of democratic status over other criteria of oppression or marginalisation. In the current debates, social conflicts continue to be defined as 'ethnic' in a far too sweeping manner. Accordingly, many architects of nation-building processes search for solutions that take account of assumed ethnicisation while other legitimate matters of concern are crossed off the political agenda and kept away from the focus of global public attention.

NOTES

1. The author thanks Isabelle Werenfels and Markus Kaiser for their very useful comments and Simone Katter for her word-processing skills.
2. 'Pluricultural' refers here to the general perception of cultural-religious diversity. 'Multicultural', in contrast, relates to representative bodies and institutions that emphasise the collective group identity and ethnic boundaries.

REFERENCES

Anderson, Benedict (1996) *Imagined Communities. Reflections on the Origins and Spread of Nationalism* (London).

Barry, Brian (2000) *Culture and Equality. An Egalitarian Critique of Multiculturalism* (Cambridge).

Elwert, Georg (1997) 'Boundaries, Cohesion and Switching. On We-Groups in Ethnic National and Religious Forms', in Hans-Rudolf Wicker (ed.),

Rethinking Nationalism and Ethnicity. The Struggle for Meaning and Order in Europe (Oxford/New York), pp. 251–72.

Gellner, Ernest (1983) *Nations and Nationalism* (Oxford).

Ghai, Yash Pal (2002) 'Constitutional Asymmetries. Communal Representation, Federalism, and Cultural Autonomy', in Andrew Reynolds (ed.), *The Architecture of Democracy. Constitutional Design, Conflict Management, and Democracy* (New York), pp. 141–70.

Gurr, Ted (1993) *Minorities at Risk. A Global View of Ethnopolitical Conflicts* (Washington, DC).

Horowitz, Donald L. (2002) 'Constitutional Design. Proposal versus Processes', in Andrew Reynolds (ed.), *The Architecture of Democracy. Constitutional Design, Conflict Management, and Democracy* (New York), pp. 15–36.

Huntington, Samuel P. (1991) *The Third Wave: Democratization in the Late Twentieth Century* (Norman, OK).

Lijphart, Arend (2002) 'The Wave of Power-Sharing Democracy', in Andrew Reynolds (ed.), *The Architecture of Democracy. Constitutional Design, Conflict Management, and Democracy* (New York), pp. 37–54.

Norris, Pippa (2002) 'Ballots Not Bullets. Testing Consociational Theories of Ethnic Conflicts, Electoral Systems, and Democratization', in Andrew Reynolds (ed.), *The Architecture of Democracy. Constitutional Design, Conflict Management, and Democracy* (New York), pp. 206–47.

Pfaff-Czarnecka, Joanna (1999) 'Debating the State of the Nation', in Joanna Pfaff-Czarnecka, Ashis Nandy, Darini Rajasingham-Senanayake and Edmund T. Gomez, *Ethnic Futures. State and Identity in Four Asian Countries* (New Delhi), pp. 41–98.

Pfaff-Czarnecka, Joanna (2001) 'Distanzen und Hierarchien. Kampf um ethnische Symbole in Nepals Öffentlichkeiten', in Alexander Horstmann and Günther Schlee (eds), *Integration durch Verschiedenheit* (Bielefeld), pp. 235–67.

Reynolds, Andrew (ed.) (2002) *The Architecture of Democracy. Constitutional Design, Conflict Management, and Democracy* (New York).

Wimmer, Andreas (2002) *Nationalist Exclusion and Ethnic Conflict. Shadows of Modernity* (Cambridge).

4
Shaping the Nation – Ideological Aspects of Nation-building

Claudia Derichs

Understood in neutral terms and without the association of fearful doctrines of political history, ideologies are systems of thought and fundamental philosophies that explain the past, present and future according to certain value models. The notion that a nation represents something that is fundamentally worth striving for is also part of the domain of ideology. In the optimum sense of economic marketing, this ideology has to be presented to the target group that needs to be convinced and which is supposed to 'buy' it. The idea that seeing themselves collectively as a nation will result in a good future for all those involved – normally the population of a state territory and its government – has to be presented to the average citizen as a product.

Nation-building involves many of the elements seen in an economic transaction at the ideological level. The main difference, however, lies in the fact that the product is not physically tangible, visible or perceptible; rather it comprises ideas that are meant to appear plausible to the 'buyers' and which they should prefer to other ideas. National cohesion must be a product that clearly surpasses the idea of separation in a divided state. Delivering the ingredients for the product design – the recipe for national identity, so to speak – is essentially the task of the government. It is responsible for spreading the 'national' idea among society because only it has the possibilities, via the central administrative machinery, to disseminate its ideas throughout the entire country in a controlled manner – with the help of the media, of course. It is quite obvious that there are organisations with competing nation-building recipes aside from the government. The government must stand its ground against these by way of better proposals (ingredients), clearly pointing out that it receives its legitimation precisely from those to whom it is now submitting its policy. As the representative of the people, the government can conceive of nation-building as a political mandate.

This chapter examines what (market) criteria the contents of a nation-building concept presented by the government have to meet in the ideological production process.

Different historical, economic, social, as well as domestic and foreign policy conditions apply in each state for initiating, continuing or concluding a nation-building process.[1] Even in clearly 'established' nations like France, England and Germany, it is still necessary to foster the national consciousness via a large number of different mechanisms of symbolic integration which go far beyond the flag and national anthem and include economic, sporting, political, historical and other elements. It is therefore questionable whether and when we can talk of an actual conclusion of nation-building. Furthermore, nation-building cannot be analysed by recording 'the state of the nation' at a certain point in time because a nation is a dynamic phenomenon and is therefore subject to constant change. A review of the various meanings and implications assumed by the 'nation' concept since 1789 – when the Third Estate in France was declared a nation by Emmanuel Joseph Sieyès (1789) – shows this in a quite impressive way. What can be examined for different epochs and different nation-states, however, is the way in which governments have 'sold' the concept of a nation to their respective populations.

PERFORMANCE CRITERIA FOR SUCCESSFUL NATION-BUILDING

In this respect, I would like to cite particular criteria that permit such an examination. In order to do this in a systematic rather than an arbitrary manner, we can borrow from the field of sociology which, although it does not have any theory on nation-building, has produced a method of examination known as 'framing'.[2] This approach can be described as a successful set of aspects that make it possible to analyse how the convictions of a small group of people can convince a large number of people through the use of specific courses of action. Applied to the subject of nation-building, this approach thus enables an insight into those things that a government should take into consideration if it wants to convince its people of the need for a national identity.[3]

A first step in this direction is to diagnose what already exists or has been achieved. In many postwar countries – for example Afghanistan or Iraq – this analysis is a sobering one: what state structures and institutions do exist are mostly relics from the time that caused deep wounds and a profound distrust of the state. The diagnosis of 'confidence in state institutions destroyed' should, therefore, lead to the prognosis of a better and more secure future (for all concerned). And things can only get better and more secure for everyone in terms of a 'national' logic if national cohesion is also guaranteed in times of crisis. Various quality characteristics are required to translate this prognosis (prospect for the future) into reality and promote national cohesion. Not least of all, the population itself has to be motivated to become involved in creating, supporting and shaping the nation. The concept of the nation therefore needs to be credible in different respects. It should

- occupy a central position among the political needs of the target groups, i.e. the population;
- have adequate scope, i.e. also play a role in the day-to-day life of the population;
- be linked to important issues on the public agenda, e.g. different policy areas;
- relate to the experiences of the target groups, e.g. incorporate traditional forms of social organisation;
- arouse narrative intimacy, i.e. have recourse to a cultural repertoire (literature, art, rituals, etc.) familiar to the people, and
- be simultaneously flexible and open to change.

If we remain with our succinct image of ideological nation-building as an economic transaction, the prognosis that 'everyone will be better off' if there is national cohesion will then become a product that the government as a vendor will offer to the population as a selected customer. This is an item that is not always easily available by virtue of its being a product that requires the cooperation of the customer before it can be made into 'what it says on the label'. This makes nation-building an interactive undertaking in a value-added process, the end-product of which has a name and vague contours, but still lacks a specific shape.

CENTRALITY AND EXTENT

A government will not be able to successfully convince its people if nation-building represents only one – and possibly a secondary – issue among many others occupying the population's attention. The subject of nation-building should, rather, occupy a central position in people's everyday political and social lives; it needs to be present, and the positive declaration of belief in a nation should be regarded as a conditio sine qua non for a better future. Applied to multiethnic states, this means, for example, convincing the population that material prosperity, inner security and a peaceful future will only be guaranteed if all ethnic groups contribute towards this and are treated as equal. A government can support this shaping of awareness via different policies.

The headwords in this regard are *centrality* and *extent*. For a population, centrality is generally given to the issue that has priority for the majority of people in the state. The nation is more a marginal rather than a central theme where different groups in society have quite different priorities which they cannot associate with the nation – a good school education for their children for some, more places for performing religious rituals for others, etc. In associating the priorities with the concept of the 'nation' – a national language and national cultural studies in the school syllabus, profession to a national religion, etc. – the issue of nation-building is assigned a central status.

The conditions to which governments have to adapt differ from state to state: in a Muslim country, it is not possible to sell pork hamburgers, no matter how appetising you make the adverts. Analogously, it is of secondary importance in many developing and threshold countries whether democracy actually is the most commendable of all political systems. The strategy of extolling nation-building as a component for the establishment of democracy will not arouse any burning national enthusiasm if two thirds of the people of a nation are threatened with starvation under democratic conditions. Or, to demonstrate this using an example: the prospect of an effective mine-clearing programme in Angola, bringing with it the possibility for families of all ethnic and social origins to farm the land again afterwards – i.e. a national effort with the government providing the resources – would make a nation-building programme more meaningful and credible than a promise to hold democratic elections.

This notion inevitably leads to the aspect of extent. Democracy is certainly a form of system that is welcomed in many societies and regarded as desirable for one's own state. However, the extent of longing for democracy often ends in the polling booth when the voters have to decide whether to elect the party that offers their children a sound school education and their families a secure income or a party that promises them democratic participation in the formulation of policies. The phenomenon of single-party dominance in numerous postcolonial countries provides clear evidence of such voting behaviour.

ASSOCIATION WITH OTHER ISSUES ON THE AGENDA

Although nation-building can occupy the number one spot on a government's political agenda, it can never stand alone, isolated in that position. The idea of associating ideological nation-building with areas of policy that can be enriched with ideological factors suggests itself, given that, in particular, nation-building does not itself represent an autonomous policy area that can be delimited; it is, rather, an extensive process that includes a large number of policy measures and which can come to the fore in quite different policy areas. Actually establishing this integration with different areas of policy is something that can be achieved, once again, primarily by the government and secondarily by the population as players in the process. A 'classic' example of associating nation-building with an important policy area is education policy. In multiethnic states with different linguistic groups, the choice of language in which lessons are taught at state schools is, for example, one of the most important decisions that a government has to make and which a population accepts or rejects: either by dismissing this decision through sending the younger generations to private schools teaching in their mother tongue (or not sending them to school at all), thus expressing their disapproval, or by accepting what is offered.

Although the government's decision to opt for a particular language as the 'national language' will rarely meet with undivided approval, justifying the choice with arguments that present as few discriminatory elements as possible and more rationally comprehensible aspects can help to decrease dissent. East Timor is a prime example of this problematic choice in that the country decided on two languages, one of which (Portuguese) is mastered only by the elite in exile and the other (Tetum) by just a minority of the population. The majority of the people (brought up in the Indonesian language) are therefore excluded from official political communication and their frustration is correspondingly high.[4] Determining the national language can thus be something far-reaching in its extent as it may exclude a number of social groups from certain forms of participation in the political process. The Arab States, on the other hand, have introduced another measure which is evidently more effective. Using modern standard Arabic as the lingua franca requires all dialectal and regional linguistic groups – with Syrian, Egyptian, Maghreb dialects, etc. – to learn that language. There is no group that speaks standard Arabic as its native language, with the result that everyone has to make the effort.

Criteria similar to those for language also apply in education policy in relation to the religious-ethical canon or for classes in regional and cultural studies. However, security, economic and social policy are likewise domains of great importance for the creation of a national identity. Allowing national defence to rest primarily on the shoulders of the politically dominant ethnic group would appear to be just as counterproductive as quota systems which do not do justice to reality and are therefore preferably circumvented. In Malaysia, for example, the much-implored quota arrangement quickly led to evasive action. The rule provides for the ethnic Malays to be given preference for company licences and business loans. So the more business-minded ethnic Chinese (more than 30 per cent of the population) simply looked around for Malay partners who were prepared to hand over their names but did not want to be bothered with management. The government's plan to turn the Malays into efficient entrepreneurs through privileges came off only in a small number of cases, virtually making nonsense of the ideology of (economic) equality for all through the introduction of quotas.

An erroneous strategic decision taken by a government can, as in this case, be tolerated over the long term and does not inevitably have to give rise to instability or other harmful consequences. It can, though, also cause a tragic backlash, as displayed by a different Malaysian example. The introduction of a favourable quota for Malays to gain access to state universities produced anything but the effect intended, with private colleges then recruiting the most able students denied entry to a state institution because of the quota. Given that the number of 'quota free-riders' is increasing at the state universities, the stoic retention of the quota system will not serve national integration in the long run or enhance national 'brain gain', especially with many graduates and academics leaving the country due to their frustration over the country's education policy. The ideology of equality is dictated to government officials in such an insistent manner in the form of the quota system it has developed into that all sight is lost of the negative consequences. Examples like this show that nation-building reaches directly into essential policy domains of state and institution-building in many areas, with the result that it cannot be regarded as an isolated task.

CONNECTING WITH THE EXPERIENCES OF TARGET GROUPS

In politics and in the business world, it is considered wise to 'collect' those who are to be convinced of something or induced to do something 'from where they are'. People with quite different backgrounds cannot suddenly be inspired by an idea, the sense of which they cannot grasp. National identity can only appear useful, meaningful or desirable as an unknown product if it links up with experiences felt to be positive in the (collective) memory of the target groups. The experience of togetherness, for instance, is associated with positive qualities in most societies. The world religions generate a sense of community by offering everyone equality before God, common striving for enlightenment or collective feeding of the faithful as a sensuous, spiritual experience.

In countries where nation-building does not proceed successfully, governments are mostly regimes without any spiritual strength or charisma, and opposition movements use this as an opportunity to fill the gap themselves. This mechanism has been used not only in Islamic states, which have attracted greater public attention over the past few decades, but also in Buddhist, Christian, Taoist and Hindu-oriented countries lacking in national cohesion. In Myanmar, the opposition leader, Aung San Suu Kyi, is the person on whom Burmese and members of other ethnic groups alike pin both their spiritual and political hopes. The military junta there has never had such charisma. This raises the question of why the junta has paid so little attention to its Buddhist-dominated neighbour, Thailand.

In Thailand, parties and prime ministers have governed for decades in the certainty that the monarch (King Bumipol) satisfies the people's yearning for spiritual leadership. Integrating the monarchy into the modern constitutional state with democratic institutions and thus connecting with the experiences, traditions and customs of the population can be seen as a strategically expedient measure. Myanmar, Algeria, China (in relation to Tibet, though also to the Cultural Revolution) and many other countries are examples of failed attempts at nation-building with policies detached from the experiences of the people.

It can rightly be asked what possibilities exist for connecting with positive experiences if the latter are something that the entire population or the majority does not have. What can you connect to in a country like present-day Iraq with a Shiite majority which endured particular suffering under the national politics of Saddam Hussein, leading to exceptionally negative experiences, without discriminating against the non-Shiites at the same time? One experience with which all sides can surely associate something positive in this case is, above all, justice. If justice is accepted as a positive experience, a government can then convincingly ensure the emergence of a legal system under which people are treated justly regardless of their ethnic, religious or cultural affiliations. In ideological terms, the value of justice confronts the principle of the law of the jungle. Achieving legal certainty therefore requires a lot of convincing through combined effort, especially among those who are supposedly stronger. It goes almost without saying that the media and a large number of creative non-state players must be given appropriate scope and the possibility to participate in this regard.

NARRATIVE FAMILIARITY

Political institutions and decision-making procedures are essentially guided by what is referred to scientifically as rational choice and appears to be supported by numerous theories – the best-known example being game theory. However, there is little about a nation that is 'rational'. It can, at least, not be institutionalised – i.e. its existence decided on or its development implemented – on the spot by a government, because this requires the approval of those who are to embody the nation in question. A nation emerges as a conceived community irrationally, as it were, since 'reason' would suggest that each member of society should look after him or herself and accept an individual or, if need be, particular (cultural, religious, ethnic, social) identity. A government wanting to sell nation-building as a recipe on the basis of rational understanding must therefore make a huge effort to get it across to the population that a national identity is intended to emerge alongside the identities that already exist (or even replace them). In brief, it must be able to demonstrate that national identity can be something very meaningful viewed in rational terms.[5]

What does a national identity provide according to rational criteria? At first sight, it does not produce wealth, glory or power and for those sacrificing themselves for the nation it can actually mean death. Nevertheless, soldiers of the national armed forces are presented in all states as those who put their lives at stake to defend national goals and interests, with such readiness portrayed as laudable, meaningful and necessary. The fallen soldiers receive praise posthumously, while power and perhaps even riches are bestowed on their generals. The essence of this – in reality, 'irrational' sacrificial behaviour being accepted, justified in rational terms ('security') and even deemed worthwhile and desirable by the 'nations' affected – lies in a narrative based on heroism and sacrifice. The narrative turns irrationality into reason, not least of all in relation to justice, where desertion, regarded by many perhaps as 'reasonable and rational', is condemned in accordance with rational juridical criteria. Virtually every culture, religion, literature and art makes use of heroes and victims (or martyrs). Studying the effect produced by this narrative is a highly interesting exercise in terms of psychology and ideational history. Its aura and capacity to arouse national feelings gives it a great appeal.

Exploiting this narrative and using it to make declaration of support for the nation into a rational matter (for example via corresponding legal codifications) is one of the most difficult steps in the process of providing the ideological interface for nation-building. PR work and persuasion of this magnitude is not something that can be done by the vendor, that is the state government, alone. It requires support from all sections of the population, the support of non-state players such as intellectuals, non-governmental organisations and representatives of the media. These are, like the rest of the population, both the subject and object of nation-building and have to carry the process in the true sense of our metaphorical image. In this process, a narrative serves to offer options for action that are familiar to the target groups. A look at Singapore illustrates this point very clearly: the extreme economic nationalism which the government there had tried hard to establish since independence (1965) did not stem from Adam Smith but, rather, from a narrative very familiar to the ethnic Chinese – and therefore 90 per cent of the population – i.e. 'the Chinese' as people with good business acumen. The media, schools as well as private and public education institutions made an important contribution towards nation-building in Singapore by virtue of their ability to communicate familiar narratives and incorporate these into the work of national integration. They performed a central role as mediator between the government and the population at large. The most important player, however, was the population itself which became involved in the economy. One of the most puzzling examples of unsuccessful nation-building, on the other hand, is South

Africa under the apartheid regime, where virtually all the narratives familiar to the majority population were either ignored or degraded by the government.

FLEXIBILITY AND OPENNESS TO CHANGE

This final aspect is hugely important because a government cannot control a state in isolation from influences of the international system or without regard to social, political and economic change internally. Change is even taking place in a country as cut off from the outside world as North Korea. The concept of nation-building founded in the promise of a better future – that is the political programme for building a nation – must be able to adapt to changes as it will otherwise lose its credibility and the motivation to work together in establishing a national identity will rapidly diminish. Theory refers in this context to 'bridging', that is building bridges between the government's political agenda and the potentially new ideational needs of society. One example of the success and, to a considerably more frequent extent, lack of success of bridging is the wave of Islamisation that has taken place since the 1970s in virtually all entirely or mainly Muslim societies. A number of states, including Malaysia, managed to integrate Islamisation and nation-building comparatively well, with Islamisation becoming embedded in the modernisation process to such an extent that no dichotomy arose between Islam and the modern age in the first place. Other countries, for example Algeria, triggered a complete erosion of confidence in the government by repressing the desire of society for a stronger Islamic identity. The protestation that such repression was 'in the national interest' was not very convincing.

A final but no less important criterion for the observations made here involves the possibility of also completely transforming the ideological framework of the 'nation' concept if need be – referred to as 'frame extension' in theoretical terminology. One example of non-transformation in this context is the case of Iran after 1979. While the population placed its confidence in the mullah government during and after the Islamic revolution with hopes of national prosperity being distributed more fairly and a 'better future for the entire nation', their expectations were not, however, fulfilled. Up to now, the ruling mullahs have still not been able to establish a political and ideological system with which the vast majority of the population (including those Iranians living in exile) can identify.

The different national leaders since Khomeini have not found any way of fundamentally transforming a system which is meeting with increasing disapproval. Although this has strengthened national awareness within the population ex negativo ('together against the government'), no common (national) identity of the clerics and society at large has emerged. The protests held in summer 2003 emphasised this point once again.

CONCLUDING REMARKS

The ability to sell the product 'nation' successfully depends on several 'comparative cost benefits'. A government which has not yet discredited itself through breach of trust or confidence has advantages over a government that has already 'cheated' its people on different occasions. It has to invest less in the credibility factor because it has not yet amassed any liabilities in this respect. To that extent, the chances for the implementation of successful nation-building were not at all bad in a large number of postcolonial countries at the time of attaining independence. Even though the national borders had been determined and arbitrarily drawn by the colonial powers, it was possible for an attractive and plausible concept of a nation to bring about the integration of different ethnic groups and cultural communities within those borders. Especially in those places where independence was preceded by a struggle for liberation there were hopes of a new beginning with a high degree of motivation to strengthen the national identity and self-assertion ('resilience').

However, the situation was and is different in countries whose populations have never yet had a genuine interest in forming a nation within the given territorial borders but have, on the contrary, been burdened for many years by fierce conflicts within their respective societies, even including civil war in some cases. The latter is true, unfortunately, for the majority of countries in which the nation-building process has proved extremely difficult up to the present time – if it is taking place at all. Orienting a nation-building strategy at least at government level to the performance criteria discussed above can be a help but cannot in itself guarantee that the process will be successful. The ideological product of 'a nation' with which the population can identify and in which it can see meaning and purpose is a product that the emergent nation creates for itself. The government should offer plausible reasons for working together on this product.

NOTES

1. The process-type nature of nation-building cannot be overemphasised. One of the most apposite comments made in this regard comes from Walker Connor (1990:99–100): 'The delay – stretched out over centuries in some cases – between the appearance of a national consciousness among those belonging to the elite and the spreading of this among the population at large reminds us of the evident but all too frequently ignored fact that nation-building is a process, and not a phenomenon or an event.'
2. A brief introduction to and discussion of this approach can be found in Hellmann and Koopmans (1998).
3. Derichs (2003) offers an example of the application of this approach to a nation-building process.
4. Portuguese and Tetum are the official languages of East Timor. Tetum is mastered by around only 30 per cent of the population. Indonesian and English are permitted as working languages.
5. Cf. Homi Bhabha's comment (1990:2): 'Shaping the nation's political "reason" as a form of narrative-textual strategies, metaphorical shifts, partial texts and figurative strategies has its own history.'

REFERENCES

Bhabha, Homi K. (ed.) (1990) *Nation and Narration* (London).
Connor, Walker (1990) 'When is a nation?', *Ethnic and Racial Studies*, Vol. 13, No. 1, pp. 92–100.
Derichs, Claudia (2003) 'Nation-Building in Malaysia: A Sociological Approach and a Political Interpretation', in Mohd Hazim Shah, K.S. Jomo and Phua Kai Lit (eds), *New Perspectives in Malaysian Studies* (Bangi, Selangor), pp. 226–48.
Hellmann, Kai-Uwe and Ruud Koopmans (eds) (1998) *Paradigmen der Bewegungsforschung* (Opladen).
Sieyès, Emmanuel Joseph (1789) *Qu'est-ce que le tiers état?* (place of publication not shown).

Part II

Case Studies

5

Deconstruction of States as an Opportunity for New Statism? The Example of Somalia and Somaliland

Wolfgang Heinrich and Manfred Kulessa

Destructive wars within individual societies have reached frightening dimensions. With the peoples affected and world peace threatened by a growing number of failed states, this is a situation that demands the attention of all countries and the international community (German Parliament, document 14/9623; Debiel 2003). The ability of a society to deal with conflicts constructively depends not least of all on its relationship with the 'state'. The breakdown of the state can also provide opportunities to create new, workable structures. These chances need to be recognised and taken advantage of for new construction. Somalia provides an example in this regard.

NATION-SAVING?

In a much-quoted article, Heldman and Ratner (1993) supported the thesis that the international community must prepare itself '... to consider a novel, expansive – and desperately needed – effort by the UN to undertake nation-saving responsibilities'. This displays a lack of differentiation in analysing complex social processes as well as a fundamental weakness with regard to recognising the systemic factors underlying the phenomenon of the failed state. The terms 'state', 'nation' and 'nation-state' are used extensively as synonyms. Heldman and Ratner speak of 'nation-saving', whereas what they really mean is 'state-saving' (Alger 1998). They assume that the cause of state failure lies in the rapid establishment of nation-states in the former colonies after the end of World War II. In fact, one of the causes for most of these crises was the creation of state structures with arbitrary borders by external players in the eighteenth and nineteenth centuries. The phenomenon of the weak and ultimately failing state is however and above all a problem of the present system of international relations (Alger 1998). In the context of this system and the role of the state in it, the failed state and the failure of any effective control of force therefore also have to be analysed.

SOVEREIGNTY, LEGITIMACY AND STATISM

According to Soerensen (1998), the political community – within the context of the nation-state in Europe, which served as a model for the creation of states on other continents – is based on material and immaterial factors. The material factors include the welfare system and guarantees of security and order by the state. The central immaterial factor is the notion of a national community substantiated by myths, historical interpretation and ideology. This political community is based on two forms of legitimacy:

- *Vertical legitimacy* denotes the relationship between society and the state and results from a general understanding that the state elite and state institutions have the right to rule on the basis of recognised values and norms in the sense of a social contract.
- *Horizontal legitimacy* defines the affiliation to the political community and marks out its boundaries (Holsti 1996). Ideally, two elements of the nation converge here: a territorially defined society within demarcated borders and the normative idea of a nationally defined community. These are the basic elements of what Holm defines as a state's 'internal sovereignty' (Holm 1998).

In Europe, this nation-state was the result of a long political development. In contrast, the African states were created by the colonial powers. The 'peoples' to whom the United Nations guaranteed the right to self-determination in 1960 lived within borders that had been drawn by others. Their notion of nation was defined in negative terms through resistance against colonial rule. Having become independent, the majority of the new states did not have any established positive concept of political community. The various attempts to construct nations subsequently proved to be failures in most cases. It was not easy to bring different groups with different languages, cultures, faiths and lifestyles together under a single national identity. Furthermore, the new state elites were very quickly tied into the political interests of their former colonial rulers or the superpowers. Staying in power and satisfying the particular interests of the groups supporting them became the primary motivation for the majority of them (Clapham 1996). The consequence of this was that the new states relied almost entirely on 'external sovereignty' resulting from recognition given by other governments. They lacked most or even all the characteristics of the much more important 'internal sovereignty' which develops from the state's success in guaranteeing human security to its citizens.

CONSTRUCTION AND DECONSTRUCTION OF STATES

States are constructed by way of social processes and politics in concrete terms. And they can be 'deconstructed' in just the same way. Looking at things this way focuses on the fact that the actors bringing a state to the point of breakdown or failure act with instrumental rationality. 'Weak' or failed states are states in different phases of deconstruction. Ernst Hillebrand (1994) distinguishes between two processes with their respective principal actors which lead to the destruction of states: a 'top down' destruction by the state elites, and the 'bottom up' process by the members of the predominantly agrarian society who are mainly oriented towards small solidarity groups. For Rainer Tetzlaff (1999) the actual mechanism that brings about the breakdown of the state is the reciprocally reinforcing effects of these two processes.

There are three categories of actors that play a particular part in state deconstruction processes:

- The *government elite* has a crucial influence on the course and outcome of nation-building processes. What is decisive is whether the government's action has a constructive impact and creates 'human security' for the citizens of the state as defined by the United Nations Development Programme (UNDP) or whether state authority, institutions and resources are misused by the members of the government elite for personal enrichment or to satisfy particular group interests. The latter erodes vertical legitimacy and weakens the state's internal sovereignty.
- The *active civil society and political forces* since the early 1990s have displayed increasing involvement, reclaiming the right of political participation. They often feel excluded from the privileges of power or involvement in processes that have a sustained effect on their lives. In many cases, these players are motivated by democratic-participative visions and the desire for public monitoring of the government's actions. Experience

shows, however, that violent disputes in the name of such ideals often do not result in any higher degree of freedom, justice or participation (Anderson 1999).

• The *non-politically active (majority of the) population* – especially in the rural regions of Africa – has only very rarely been able to boast any positive experiences with the state. Essential social services have frequently been provided by private bodies or within the context of self-help. The conventional security sector too often has been characterised by arbitrary arrests, human rights violations and corruption to such an extent that the citizens have had to protect themselves against the state rather than it protecting them. It is therefore no surprise when broad sections of the population decide to use the 'exit option', seeking to avoid contact with the state institutions and withdrawing into the private sphere and the informal sector (Cheru 1988).

FROM DECONSTRUCTION TO RECONSTRUCTION

Crisis, as in the Chinese scripture, is formed from elements of risk and opportunity and can, in positive cases, lead to a constructive new beginning that leaves behind the legacy of colonial and postcolonial eras, and enables the community to organise its affairs in a more dependable and participative manner. Besides chaos, the destruction stage can also trigger processes of reflection and liberation. If deconstruction of the state is the result of instrumentally rational action, it is then obvious that such processes cannot be reversed by a simple 'reconstruction' of the state, that is a return to the status quo ante. The challenge is, rather, that of renewed construction of society and the state, which can establish a national identity and constitute internal sovereignty.

Comparative studies in crisis regions have shown that people do not live in a political and administrative vacuum after the breakdown of state structures and functions; rather communities fall back on other structures and mechanisms in order to resolve necessary matters of common concern (Bryden 1995; Anderson 1999). Traditional ways are rekindled or other institutions such as local groups and non-governmental organisations (NGOs) take on political and administrative responsibilities.

It is generally easier to establish the bond of loyalty that unites citizens at the local and regional level. At the national level it is essential for the vast majority of the population not to have any doubts or reservations about belonging to the state's political community (Rustow 1970). The national identity must permit differentiation, e.g. according to religious, ethnic or social criteria, though these do not have to lead to the political community being called into question in fundamental terms.

SOMALIA: A STATE IN DECONSTRUCTION

Soon after the Italian and British colonial territories in Somalia had achieved their independence in 1960, they voluntarily joined together to form the Republic of Somalia. The colonial era had bestowed the modern centralised state on Somalian society. The new form of social organisation conflicted sharply with the traditional, radically egalitarian social structure of the Somalis, which Lewis (1961) described as a 'pastoral democracy'. In contrast to most settled societies, it has virtually no formally institutionalised authority. Beyond the family unit, relations within society are very flexible and depend on the situation. The social structure of the Somalis can be described as a network of extensively autonomous family units integrated into alliances at many levels (clans, subclans and further subdivisions).

In the initial years of independence, Somalia was regarded as a model democracy in Africa, with numerous parties standing for election, mostly on a clan basis. Between 1961 and 1969, various elected governments alternated with each other. Like no other country in Africa, Somalia was seen as a nation-state whose citizens belonged predominantly to one people with the same language and religion. On the other hand, the young state's foreign policy was characterised from the outset by the desire to unite all regions inhabited by Somalis in Ethiopia, Djibouti and Kenya, which led to conflicts with the neighbouring countries, the effects of which are still felt today.

On 21 October 1969, General Siad Barre came to power as the result of a coup d'état. His government's declared goal was to create a modern nation-state based on the socialist model. A single-party system was introduced and clan loyalty denounced as backward and primitive. Over the years, the ruling party built up a comprehensive system of control and an authoritarian, overcentralised governmental regime. Somalia's citizens increasingly experienced the state as a repressive system offering no framework for identification. Observers were reminded of a colony under foreign military occupation (Lewis 1991). As a result the Somalis turned more and more to their clan groups that ensured survival rather than the state's social systems. Although it condemned clan loyalty, the Siad Barre government was founded on a clan basis from the very outset; and it was Siad Barre's clan in particular that benefited from development aid and foreign trade relations. With growing dissatisfaction and opposition, the regime's political base narrowed to an ever-increasing extent.

In 1978, opposition groups in north-west Somalia, the former British protectorate, began to organise resistance against the repressive central government. In an effort to destroy their organisational base, the regime waged a brutal war against the civilian population. Towns and villages were bombarded, wells and waterholes poisoned and destroyed, cattle seized and human rights violated in a grave and systematic manner. During the civil war, the official economy almost completely collapsed.

The Siad Barre regime is a classic example of a policy that placed state preservation before nation-building – practising the former with ruthless force where deemed necessary. Whereas the regime had initially pursued a policy of modernising the state and society via extending the education system and providing social services and a modern administration, over the years it was the preservation of power itself that became the core of its policy. The regime attempted to achieve this via clan loyalty and integration into the geopolitical interests of the superpowers. However, the state's internal sovereignty eroded to a point where the government could only stay in power through external support, the cooperation of other clans and the use of massive force.

The opposition forces eventually managed to drive the government army out of the north-west. On 27 January 1991, Siad Barre's military dictatorship finally collapsed. This ended the formal existence of the state of Somalia which had, however, already become an empty shell many years before, providing its citizens with neither security nor social services. It had been able to exist for many years only because other governments recognised the despotic regime and supported it regardless of its systematic and massive violation of human rights.

A time of chaos followed the collapse of the dictatorship in which warlords and their militias fought for territories, supremacy and control of economic resources. The forces that had ousted Siad Barre and his regime from power were not able to form a new government.

International intervention, initially under the leadership of the USA and then in the form of a UN mission (UNOSOM), proved ineffective to a great extent and was discontinued after three years. The world community had to realise that state-building after war required the cooperation of local communities and their structures and could only be successful if pursued 'from the bottom up'.

RECONSTRUCTION OF THE STATE

Although a number of warlords are still struggling for power over a decade after the fall of the Siad Barre regime, there are also numerous regions where local communities have ended violence and where local and semi-state authorities are functioning effectively (Menkhaus 1996). In the north, two autonomous regional entities have emerged – the Republic of Somaliland and Puntland – which have functioning administrations and a considerable measure of security. The situation is similar for parts of the region of south-west Somalia (Heeger 2003:216).

During the time of the UN intervention, a local administration was set up under an Islamic-Somalian court in the northern part of the capital, Mogadishu, which was successful in creating a relatively peaceful zone. This is the base of the transitional national government (TNG) established by a peace conference in Arta (Djibouti) in 2000 which, although it claims to be national, has not been able to achieve recognition throughout the entire country.

Further conferences on reconciliation and national rapprochement have taken place in Kenya. The neighbouring countries officially supporting the peace negotiations under the umbrella of the Intergovernmental Authority on Development (IGAD) are, however, pursuing their own interests, which by no means always correspond to the aspirations of the Somali people for a unified nation. It is possible that the solution of the Somalia problem will only be found in the long term within the framework of a union of states in the Horn of Africa. But the chances of this happening are not particularly favourable at present.

It is important to note here that the civil war was fought most intensively at the interfaces of international trade, that is in the ports where fuel, electronics and weapons enter the country, in those areas where goods are produced for export, and in the capital, Mogadishu. In other regions, traditional persons of authority assumed responsibility for security and the survival of the local communities.

This accomplishment should not be underestimated in view of a deeply divided society and the lack of state authority (Farah 1994).

More than a dozen peace conferences have been held since 1992 with international assistance. Most of these conferences followed the classic diplomatic model involving only the representatives of the parties actively involved in waging war. There is one important exception: in March 1993, the UN Secretary-General's Special Envoy Mohamed Sahnoun was able to persuade the UN to involve a large number of representatives of Somalian civil society as observers in the peace conference held in Addis Ababa. Their participation was supported by non-governmental organisations, especially the Swedish Life and Peace Institute (LPI). Outside the official negotiations the representatives of civil society were able to exert influence on the discussion and the outcome of the conference. Although signed by the warring parties only, the Addis Ababa Agreement of March 1993 did provide the framework for establishing administrative structures at local, district and provincial level as part of a provisional government structure. The building of these new self-administration structures is so far the only concrete result of the numerous peace conferences organised by the UN.

LPI and UNOSOM followed Somalian tradition when they invited the leading personalities of the communities concerned (chiefs, elders, religious leaders) to public meetings at which the establishment of administrative councils were to be discussed and decided on. The bodies set up in this way are not, however, a reproduction of the 'traditional' Somali structure of rule, which does not have any formally institutionalised authority. An attempt was made, rather, to combine the requirements of a modern state system with traditional forms of decision-making (Heinrich 1997).

Occasionally, the elders and traditional leaders became members of the councils, though in most cases they preferred to remain on the outside as independent authorities. In the Republic of Somaliland, the elders form a type of constitutional court in the *Guurti* in addition to the government institutions. In a few cases the new councils have also contributed to conflicts, e.g. in the dispute surrounding the involvement of local groups or concerning the influence of the warring parties, which have sometimes interfered to a great extent. On occasions, literate refugees from the capital managed to capture dominant positions. In the majority of cases, however, the councils are proving to be effective institutions for participative management of local matters, though traditional clan authorities continue to be entrusted with the settlement of local conflicts in accordance with the old customs. In the meantime, the councils have become the centrepiece of a functioning system of local self-administration. Starting points and partners can be found here for international development cooperation, from the UNDP's wide-ranging Somalia Rehabilitation Programme (SRP) to NGO activities.

THE EXAMPLE OF SOMALILAND

Somaliland, 'the nation that nobody knows' (*The Economist*, 14.4.2001), quite evidently meets the conditions of modern statism. It was formed in 1993 on the basis of a broad participatory process. The state and its institutions have internal sovereignty through the approval of the population numbering 2 million people. The state bodies safeguard peace and a relatively high degree of human security. The two chambers of parliament are constituted by democratic election and the government and the opposition have developed relationships of constructive political competition. There is an independent judiciary, an active civil society, a critical press and security forces that are subject to public control. The state has its own currency and central bank, an international airport and seaport, as well as a flourishing private economy extensively free of regulation.

Nonetheless, the Republic of Somaliland has not yet been recognised by any other country. The so-called international community argues that it is impossible to change the colonial borders and that the 'national unity' of Somalia has to be protected. The lack of conceptual clarity referred to above has a fatal impact in this case because what the international community is concerned with here is not a matter of 'national' unity but, rather, the preservation of territorial unity. The line of argument put forward by the government of Somaliland in this context is well-founded in historical terms. It argues that after the disintegration of the unified state, the people of the former British colonial territory are back to the situation during the days of independence when Somaliland, having been freed from British rule, existed as an independent state for four days in June 1960 before joining together with the region of the former Italian colony to constitute the Republic of Somalia as the result of a voluntary resolution passed by its parliament.

There is good reason to assume that international recognition of Somaliland would be beneficial for peace and development in Somalia as well as the entire region. A state has been built there, the structure of which is based on a successful combination of tradition and modern democratic structures, thus enabling it to enjoy a high degree of internal sovereignty – very much in contrast to the transitional national government in Mogadishu, which entirely lacks internal sovereignty and is exclusively dependent on being recognised and supported by foreign states. It would therefore be in the interests of long-term peaceful development in the region for the Republic of Somaliland to be recognised internationally in parallel with the peace endeavours for Somalia and to receive aid and economic cooperation – also in view of the forthcoming elections.

PROSPECTS FOR SOMALIA

Negotiations to resolve the stalemate in Somalia have been going on again in Kenya since October 2002 mediated by the Kenyan government on behalf of IGAD. It can hardly be expected that these talks will result in a breakthrough leading to an agreement that would provide the basis for a widely accepted government and the building of a new state of Somalia, even though a capable mediator has been found in the person of the experienced Kenyan diplomat Bethuel Kiplagat. There are three main reasons for this scepticism regarding success: the lack of representativeness of the parties involved, the lack of readiness by the powers-that-be to accept an overall concept, and political interests on the part of the neighbouring countries and the USA.

The development of the private sector has amazed many observers (Heeger 2003:224). Somalian entrepreneurs have demonstrated that shipping, telecommunications and airlines can evidently be organised without state structures – as long as there is no interference from an outside government. The Somalis felt the full force of the latter when the US administration froze the assets of the largest employer, al Barakaat, a finance and trading company, and thousands of Somalis were deprived of their incomes. The Somalian diaspora used to remit around €500 million a year to their families via this company. Even though the owners of al Barakaat were able to have their accounts freed by US courts, thus avoiding an economic catastrophe, Somalia is repeatedly suspected of harbouring terrorists because of prejudices and the fact that Islam is practised there (Aden 2002, 2003).

The Somalis cannot do without building a new state. This is also something that should seriously interest its neighbours and the international community. The experience of the past few years has shown that no international conference will be able to formulate a solution that fulfils the high expectation of the Somalis as long as only or primarily the 'war actors' are involved in the negotiations. What is needed, as Aden (2000:109) puts it, are 'visionary realists' because the need here is to support developed and developing approaches towards a new form of statism. The Republic of Somaliland deserves international recognition, assistance, advice and encouragement on the way to establishing a federal constitution which can promote peaceful relations – just like the other regional structures and local councils in Somalia.

SUMMARY

After extensive deconstruction of the state, a distinction has to be made between nation-building and state-building. The case of Somalia shows that, before the state can be constructed again, the society has to be built to form a 'political community' in the sense of Soerensen (1998): 'National identity establishes a bond of loyalty, it helps create the minimum of national unity which is at the core of the political community.' If 'national identity' is a bond of loyalty that binds together the citizens of a state to form a community, a certain measure of national consciousness is then a necessary prerequisite for the construction of a state and building a democratic system of governance.

Political and administrative structures performing state functions must be built on the basis of a 'political community'. Procedures for the establishment of institutions and the selection of personnel will only be workable if they are based on the fundamental consensus of a 'political community'. At the same time, protection and further development of the 'national identity' in the sense of a generally shared consciousness of being part of the political community, are a necessary addition for the development and preservation of effective state structures and institutions.

The deconstruction phase of a state can lead to a building period. Civil society actors and economic initiatives can make important contributions in this regard. International diplomacy and political science can obtain important insights from the experience of the Somalis into how a new beginning can grow out of crisis.

REFERENCES

Aden, Abdurahman (2000) *Von der Trommel zum Handy* (Bad Honnef).

Aden, Abdurahman (2002) 'Somalia ist nicht Bin Ladens Land', *epd-Entwicklungspolitik* No. 1/2002, pp. 36–8.

Aden, Abdurahman (2003) 'Vor Allah sind alle Somali gleich', *Le Monde Diplomatique/TAZ* (January).

Alger, Chadwick F. (1998) *Failed States and the Failure of States: Self-Determination, States, Nations and Global Governance* (Paper presented at the International Conference 'Failed States and International Security: Causes, Prospects, and Consequences', Purdue University, West Lafayette, 25–27 February).

Anderson, Mary B. (1999) *Do No Harm. How Aid Can Support Peace – Or War* (Boulder, CO).

Bryden, Matt (1995) 'Somalia: The Wages of Failure', *Current History*, Vol. 49, No. 591, pp. 145–51.

Cheru, Fantu (1988) *Beyond the Debt Crisis: Rethinking Development in Africa* (International Studies in Sociology and Social Anthropology) (place of publication not shown).

Clapham, Christopher (1996) *Africa and The International System. The Politics of State Survival* (Cambridge).

Debiel, Tobias (2003) 'Staatsversagen, Gewaltstrukturen und blockierte Entwicklung: Haben Krisenländer noch eine Chance?', *Aus Politik und Zeitgeschichte*, No. 13–14/2003, pp. 15–23.

Farah, Ahmed Yussuf (1994) *The Roots of Reconciliation. Peace Making Endeavours of Contemporary Lineage Leaders: A Survey of Grassroots Peace Conferences in 'Somaliland'* (London).

Heeger, Carsten (2003) 'Somaliland (Somalia): Staatszerfall, Staatenbildung und Friedenskonsolidierung', in Mir A. Ferdowsi and Volker Matthies (eds), *Den Frieden gewinnen. Zur Konsolidierung von Friedensprozessen in Nachkriegsgesellschaften* (ONE World series from the Development and Peace Foundation No. 15, Bonn), pp. 208–37.

Heinrich, Wolfgang (1997) *Building The Peace. Experiences of Collaborative Peacebuilding in Somalia 1993–1996* (Horn of Africa Series 3, Life and Peace Institute, Uppsala).

Heldman, Gerald B. and Steven R. Ratner (1993) 'Saving Failed States', *Foreign Policy*, Vol. 89, pp. 3–20.

Hillebrand, Ernst (1994) 'Zivilgesellschaft und Demokratie in Afrika', *Internationale Politik und Gesellschaft*, No. 1, pp. 57–71.

Holm, Hans-Henrik (1998) *The Responsibility That Will Not Go Away. Weak States in the International System* (Paper presented at the International Conference 'Failed States and International Security: Causes, Prospects, and Consequences', Purdue University, West Lafayette, 25–27 February).

Holsti, Kalevi J. (1996) *The State, War, and the State of War* (Cambridge).

Lewis, I.M. (1991) 'The Recent Political History of Somalia', in Kim Barcik and Sture Normark (eds), *Somalia – A Historical, Cultural And Political Analysis* (Uppsala).

Lewis, I. M. (1961) *A Pastoral Democracy* (London).

Life and Peace Institute (1991) *Somalia* (Uppsala).

Menkhaus, Ken (1996) 'Putting It Back Together Again', *New Routes,* Vol. 1, No. 3, pp. 18–21.

Rustow, Dankwart A. (1970) 'Transitions to Democracy', *Comparative Politics*, Vol. 2, No. 3, pp. 337–65.

Soerensen, Georg (1998) *Democratization in the Third World. The Role of Western Politics and Research* (Paper presented at the Conference 'Failed States and International Security: Causes, Prospects, and Consequences', Purdue University, West Lafayette, 25–27 February).

Tetzlaff, Rainer (1999) 'Der Wegfall effektiver Staatsgewalt in den Staaten Afrikas', *Die Friedenswarte*, Vol. 74, No. 3, pp. 307–30.

6
Afghanistan: Nation-building in the Shadow of the Warlords and the 'War on Terror'

Rangin Dadfar Spanta

Reporting on Afghanistan currently focuses on the successes of the Afghan government and international politics since the fall of the Taliban – and, indeed, the situation in Afghanistan is certainly better today than it was. In 2003, there were 5 million Afghan children attending school; around 150 publications have established themselves as daily newspapers or periodicals in Kabul; assistance is provided by more than 1,200 registered non-governmental organisations (NGOs), and international security troops attempt to guarantee calm and order in Kabul within the framework of the International Security Assistance Force Afghanistan (ISAF).

These changes are elements of an overall problem that is more complex than is often perceived in the web of hegemonic US interests and the international community's pressure to provide justification. The declared policy presently being pursued in relation to Afghanistan displays an abundance of deficiencies, indicating a great lack of properly thought-out postwar concepts. This chapter examines the essential features of the political, economic and social situation as well as the problems of state-building in Afghanistan.

THE GOVERNMENT IN KABUL: A FRAGILE STRUCTURE

Since June 2002, the new government in Kabul has been known as the 'Islamic Transitional Government of Afghanistan'. It is led by Hamid Karzai and is made up of the different groups that took part in the first Petersberg Afghanistan Conference held in December 2001. It comprises more than 40 persons holding ministerial or equivalent positions plus a number of representatives of the President and his advisers.

The justification for these groups sharing power lies in the assumption that they still have heavily armed squads or are members of the 'American team' (see below) representing the interests of their ethnic groups. This politicisation of the ethnic factor in Afghanistan is pursued both by the warlords and the international players. In the absence of democratic legitimation and a countrywide power base, it is extremely problematic to explain the power of the warlords through anything other than military strength.

In the Afghan government, a distinction can be made – in simplified terms – between four factions, though these do not have uniform internal structures:

The 'American team': the Afghan exiles

The 'American team' predominantly consists of Afghan exiles who have returned from the US and have the American government to thank for their positions. This group plays a more important role at the international level and in the diplomatic arena than it does inside the country. With many Afghans assuming that this faction was the only alternative to the Islamists within the government or the warlords, it initially had the sympathy of the population. However, as it became clear that it was unable to ensure the stability and reconstruction of the country, its popularity waned. This group is not able to assert itself against the warlords and Islamists. Its position is being substantially weakened by the absence of its own military and organisational possibilities, the long period spent in exile by its members, as well as the reduction of the 'war on terror' to the military option.

The 'Supervisory Council' faction: the group of the former commander, Ahmad Shah Masoud

The 'Supervisory Council' (Shura-i Nezar) was established by Commander Ahmad Shah Masoud during the Afghan resistance against the Soviet Union (1979–89) as a coordinating body for the military activities of the Mujaheddin in the Panshir valley region, the areas to the north of Kabul and a number of provinces in northern Afghanistan. It consisted for the most part of Mujaheddin of the 'Islamic society' (Jemat i Islami Afghanistan), the party of the subsequent state president, Rabani. The 'Supervisory Council' became increasingly significant and formed the main force in the northern alliance after the Mujaheddin government had been driven out of Kabul by the Taliban in 1996. Following the Petersberg Afghanistan Conference, leading personalities of the 'Supervisory Council' constituted the most important pillar of the Afghan transitional government.

The group is a military and political organisation that emerged from the radical Islamist movement of Afghanistan and which, although it conducts itself moderately at times and moves away from fundamentalist positions, continues to insist on the establishment of a state founded on Islamic law. It controls the Ministries of Defence, Foreign Affairs, Education and Higher Education, as well as the secret service and other key positions. Its representatives have good military organisations at their disposal, asserting their interests by means of intimidation and force. The 'Supervisory Council' is one of the main factors in the fragmentation of Afghanistan today. Its organisational possibilities, its strong position in the government and its influence in the regions run by the warlords enable it to consolidate its power base. While the Minister of Defence heads the 'Commission for the Formation of an Impartial Army', he is at the same time recruiting former Mujaheddin fighters under the name of 'Holy War Squads' (Ghundha-i Jehadi) for a paramilitary group following the Iranian model of the guardians of the revolution. Paradoxically, he also benefits from financial assistance through the 'antiterror alliance'.

Representatives of regional and local warlords in the central government

The representatives of local warlords, who are close to the faction referred to above, form a pact with the powerful faction of the Mujaheddin within the government while the militarily less powerful representatives of the militia, belonging more to the Hazara and Uzbek ethnic groups, move closer to either of the groups mentioned depending on the situation. They act as the long arms of the powerful and less powerful decentralised warlords, who come mainly from the regions of central and eastern Afghanistan and are not particularly influential in the capital, Kabul.

Regional and local warlords

The real rulers outside Kabul are the warlords and they have constantly extended their military power since the fall of the Taliban. The so-called disarmament process, which is being carried out very hesitantly, primarily benefits the more powerful warlords, who are gaining ever-greater control of their territories and recruiting their own armed units.

The paradox of the policy pursued by the international players lies in the fact that it calls for and wants to help strengthen the central government while, at the same time, supporting the warlords by way of financial benefits. The example of the Khost region – where the governor nominated by the Karzai government is engaged in a struggle with his predecessor who, on the other hand, is supported financially by the US – demonstrates that the US first gears its policy to the military requirements of the war on terror and, second, does not have any long-term strategy for the country. This conflicting policy can be observed in all regions of Afghanistan. Propagating respect for human rights on the one hand, the US simultaneously supports the warlords in the north of the country, who are known to have committed war crimes.

This intensifies the asymmetry of power between Kabul and the regions as a source of conflict, with the positions of the 'top dogs' (Galtung 1997:63), that is the warlords and the Mujaheddin faction in the government, being strengthened vis-à-vis the 'underdogs'.

ECONOMIC ACTIVITIES

Warfare is still a lucrative occupation in Afghanistan. A generation that grew up in a war and has learnt nothing other than to wage war is only too pleased to place its military skills at the disposal of the warlords and the 'antiterror alliance'. Both these 'employers' pay their soldiers and fighters more than a university professor gets, for example. Despite the talk of disarmament, a 'political economy of arms' has emerged: carrying weapons and using them to demonstrate power has become something quite natural, although the ordinary people would like to be freed from the 'shadow of the Kalashnikov'.

The production of opium and opium derivatives has increased again in Afghanistan. According to a report by the BBC (26.6.2003), opium production for 2003 was predicted to be 19 times higher than that in 2001. The fight against drugs is unsuccessful owing to the government's executive possibilities being limited and because it does not have control of many parts of the country. The ongoing war on terror in the south creates opportunities for opium production and a large number of the local rulers also make money from the trafficking of drugs. There is a broad network of international drug dealers whose contacts extend via Iran and Central Asia to the European continent.

The smuggling of luxury goods is another source of income. They are imported into Afghanistan via the Arab Emirates, subjected to very low customs duty and then exported as contraband mainly to Pakistan, earning money for the Afghan dealers, the warlords and the central government. This means that, in addition to the warlords and drug barons, those dealing in consumer and luxury goods also have a superior position – a fact that political observers do not take appropriate account of.

Despite the huge presence of international organisations and grand proclamations by international politicians, nothing has so far been done with regard to reconstructing the extensively devastated industrial sector. Agricultural production is still below capacity, suffering from the consequences of a four-year drought, destruction of the irrigation systems, the laying of mines in large areas of the country and a lack of qualified workers. Food production is also unattractive for the population in view of the lucrative drug trade luring farmers to cultivate poppies rather than edible crops. On top of this, prices for agricultural products are being squeezed as a result of the international programmes to combat hunger and the distribution of food to returning Afghan refugees.

INTERNATIONAL INTERVENTION AND STATE-BUILDING IN AFGHANISTAN

In the discourse on failed states, the terms 'state-building' and 'nation-building' are frequently used synonymously. However, they are not one and the same thing. The lack of clarity of the terminology leads to confusion in defining other terms such as 'state-nation', 'cultural nation,' 'nation' as a people's community or 'nation' as a legal definition, i.e. as a society of citizens.

In the debate relating to Afghanistan, it is, in my view, a matter of establishing a nation-state, ensuring the state's monopoly of force over the entire territory and building an efficient national economy. Furthermore, establishment of the rule of law and extensive democratisation of the state can also be put on the agenda where a normative approach is applied.

The state-building project has been underway since the end of 2001. The international players include, in descending order of their relevance, the US, the UN, the neighbouring states of Afghanistan, the NGOs and the European Union. The basic idea according to which the government was put together at the first Petersberg Conference in 2001 was that Afghanistan was a multiracial state and the military groups, warlords and Afghan exiles sharing in government were to represent their ethnic groups or, as frequently formulated in the media, their tribes. The 'multiethnic government' resulted. Its democratic legitimation was to be underpinned by the inclusion of the tribal council, the *loya jirga*, meeting in Kabul in June 2002 as the traditional institution of the Afghan tribes.

In fact, this construct does not take account of the social change that has taken place in Afghan society over the past 30 years and possesses a somewhat distorted view of its realities. It also misunderstands the population's real expectations. This is the reason for the social basis and social legitimation of the state being and remaining so fragile and weak.

DESTRUCTION OF THE TRADITIONAL LEGITIMATION OF AFGHAN SOCIETY

The traditional tribal structures of Afghanistan have been permanently damaged; their instruments – like the traditional *loya jirga* – are not suitable for solving modern conflicts or for state-building. Afghanistan's local traditions have never been embedded countrywide. The traditional *loya jirga* has never been an instrument for expressing the will of the people; it is, rather, a power-stabilising mechanism with local and tribal legitimation. Nonetheless, conditions have been created through the holding of the *loya jirga* which have normative power.

Like the course of the war and the resistance, the consequences of these have also been inconsistent over the last 24 years. Despite the huge devastation, Afghanistan's society has become emancipated in a number of respects.

The reforms undertaken by the 'Democratic People's Party of Afghanistan' (1978–92) and the Soviet invasion (1979–89) met with resistance from the country's traditional structures and authorities. According to the Soviet communist version, Afghanistan was a feudal society that needed to be transformed. The proclaimed class struggle grew in intensity and brutality with the state interventions following the April coup of 1978. The state authority was supposed to change and reorganise production conditions and ownership rights (Sigrist 1986; Grevemeyer 1987; Dadfar Spanta 1993). The fact was, however, that the class conditions postulated by the Soviet communists did not exist in Afghanistan. Their policy was therefore out of touch with reality, while the attempts to implement it regardless were all the more brutal.

Land reform failed because Afghanistan did not have the large-scale land-holding tradition encountered in feudal societies (Roy 1985; Grevemeyer 1987). A class confrontation mobilising the peasants under the banner of Soviet communist reform methods did not take place because traditional and kinship loyalties were stronger than class antagonism. Literacy failed because those concerned would not allow themselves to be made mere objects of a campaign. In a country where values like 'honour' stand above everything else, it was impossible to send peasant women to ideologically oriented literacy classes by decree in order to establish a Soviet–Afghan brotherhood.

In attempting to snatch control of society's interests away from the traditional leadership, the Afghan state exceeded its limitations. Traditional consensus, which had come about through an historically evolved, political and social sharing of tasks between the decentralised tribal powers and the central government, collapsed. The initial spontaneous uprisings by the population transpired primarily on the basis of traditional loyalties.

The traditional elites were either eliminated by the political interventions of the 'Democratic People's Party of Afghanistan' and the Soviet army or they proved to be incompetent during the resistance. Over the course of the war, a new leadership class formed, with skills that were indispensable for modern warfare. Qualities like organisational talent and propaganda skills were of special significance in this respect. The dominance of the traditional elite was thus undermined and partially done away with. This social policy development is of particular relevance for the attempt at conflict management and state-building in today's Afghanistan.

Given that the traditional institutions are severely damaged and out of accord with the new balance of power, all endeavours aimed at state-building in Afghanistan with the principal help of the tradition that has remained are faced with the fact that it is not primarily the tribal leadership but, rather, a new military and political elite that now has the say. These new elites do not necessarily have any traditional, tribal legitimation; most of the leaders are not representatives of their ethnic groups. They lack both traditional as well as modern legitimation in that they do not represent their 'tribes' or have any ethnically related organisations or political representations that express the common political interests of the respective ethnic groups. Most of the factions and persons sharing power do not comprise traditional tribal leaders; instead they are made up of military commanders, leaders of Islamic parties or representatives of foreign lobbies. This also applies to President Karzai as well as his rivals inside and outside the government.

INADEQUATE APPROACHES BY EXTERNAL POLITICAL PLAYERS

The state-building endeavours of the international players in Afghanistan suffer from conceptional problems and do not display any uniform strategy. While the US makes its overall policy dependent on the military requirements of the war on terror – also seeking close cooperation with the warlords in this respect – and sees the state-building project as pushing through the principles of a neoliberal market economy, the Europeans, especially Germany, place their faith in the NGOs. This means that an attempt is being made to accomplish state-building with inappropriate instruments and players acting against each other.

Furthermore, coordination between the policy of the international peace-keeping forces, US military action and the civil activities referred to as peace-building is far from adequate. Peace-keeping and peace-building activities are frequently carried out side by side, with the result that their effect is lost.

The declared goal of the international community is to strengthen the central government, enabling it to assert its monopoly of force throughout the country and carry out its responsibilities. However, its power is very limited, restricted primarily by that of the warlords, who are paradoxically supported by the US. US state-building policy in Afghanistan is evidently secondary to the requirements of the military actions against al Qaeda and the remaining Taliban.

However, a policy aimed at bringing about reconstruction mainly through NGOs also causes problems that impede the state-building process. Development cooperation funding is privatised when routed mostly via NGOs. The NGOs from the north are performing an increasing number of public functions which are the classic domain of a government. Resources for necessary long-term undertakings are used by NGOs for projects with a short time span. Larger projects of particular importance for the national economy – road-building, education, healthcare, dam construction, power stations and mining projects – have up to now been the classic responsibilities of the state. As long as the NGOs spend most of the reconstruction funding on their small and local projects, the country's devastated infrastructure will remain weak or dysfunctional.

The presence of the NGOs in Afghanistan is, nonetheless, essential. Despite all the justified criticism (Medico International 2002), they carry out remarkable work in fighting hunger and disasters as well as in the area of human rights protection. What they cannot accomplish, nor can it be expected of them, are the tasks of state-building and the setting-up of state institutions.

Afghan society is being permanently paralysed by ethnic fragmentation, corruption and nepotism, as well as the toleration of private armies. There is broad consensus that these factors have become the most significant obstacles to state-building. It should be equally clear that strengthening the political power elite in the present government or the warlords cannot be the solution to the problems.

PROSPECTS FOR CONFLICT MANAGEMENT AND PEACE

In order to reduce the warlords' possibilities for asserting their power interests and strengthen the central government's chances for exerting administrative control, it is important to break the dominance of the former and reorganise the composition of the latter. The state-building process will not be able to succeed without the comprehensive disarmament of the military groups of Afghanistan's different rulers and militias or without the social integration of those who see warfare as a normal job.

The country urgently needs an impartial and non-partisan transitional government which stands above the ethnic groups and has the necessary professional as well as political and moral competence. Creating the conditions for a functioning state could be possible in a transitional phase with a government of capable, democratically oriented technocrats backed up by the international community, including the presence of ISAF in the cities and major towns. Without these conditions and in the absence of disarming and getting rid of the private armies, standardising legal norms and extending the state's monopoly of force over the entire territory, elections and other political mechanisms will only serve to strengthen the power of the warlords and encourage denationalisation of the state of Afghanistan.

Furthermore, the country urgently needs the development of democratic structures. Without the creation of participative possibilities for the population and the furthering of organisational opportunities for its citizens, Afghanistan will increasingly develop into a place of enrichment for individuals and the repressive safeguarding of interests and privileges enjoyed by the warlords and Mujaheddin parties. Building state structures and strengthening the central government with its executive bodies are of particular importance. This process can only be successful, however, if civil society is supported and strengthened at the same time. It is therefore essential to promote the involvement of the population in building the country. Despite the forced politicisation of the ethnic factor, there is no separatist movement in Afghanistan. This and the will of many citizens for their own Afghanistan are positive elements that facilitate reorganisation of the Afghan nation within a federal structure.

State-building in Afghanistan is directly linked to stability, development and ensuring peace. It must be clearly evident that peace is something worthwhile. This requires an overall strategy that takes equal account of the elements of state-building, the economy, the social situation, the environment and peace. Any one-sided emphasis on a single component will create further problems now and for the future.

The US and its allies were successful in the war against the Taliban and al Qaeda in the first phase; now, however, they run the risk of losing the 'big one at Hindu Kush' (Kleveman 2002:254). The superpower has justified its intervention with the objectives of eradicating terrorism as well as stabilising, reconstructing and democratising the country. Afghanistan should not, as the Bush administration put it, remain a base for terrorism and fundamentalism.

More than two years have passed since then and developments are now going in a different direction. Military incursions and acts of sabotage by the remaining Taliban and al Qaeda in the south and east of the country are constantly on the increase. Groups operating from Pakistan carry out attacks on Afghan soil and then use the country as a retreat. The latest elections in the border regions between Pakistan and Afghanistan were won by the Pakistani Islamists. Pakistan, the only atomic power among the Islamic nations, is more unstable than ever, with the country's political elite deeply divided by different ethnic and ideological orientations. Islam as the principal ideological element for justifying the existence of the Pakistani nation is no longer able to guarantee the unity of that country.

Afghanistan is a conglomerate of ethnic groups which maintain close relations with the same ethnic groups in the bordering countries of Pakistan, Uzbekistan, Turkmenistan and Tajikistan. These are postcolonial states displaying all the relevant concomitants, with the Central Asian states – allies of the US in the war on terror – representing prime examples of contemporary tyranny without democratic legitimation. They have unstable state structures with Islamist and ethnically oriented opposition movements as well as major economic and social problems. Furthermore, the struggle for power in this region is concentrated between the US, Russia, China and Iran. Any collapse of Afghanistan would trigger a crisis directly threatening all the neighbouring countries. If the Afghanistan crisis were to escalate further, the conflicts in the neighbouring states and the whole of Central Asia would threaten stability and world peace more than ever. Nation-building and the establishment of a functioning nation-state in Afghanistan will therefore decide not only the future of the Afghans, but that of the entire region. There is still time for the international community to correct its dubious course.

REFERENCES

Dadfar Spanta, Rangin (1993) *Afghanistan, Entstehung der Unterentwicklung, Krieg und Widerstand* (Frankfurt/M.).

Galtung, Johan (1997) 'Theorien des Friedens', in Berthold Meyer (ed.), *Formen der Konfliktregelung* (Opladen), pp. 55–64.

Grevemeyer, Jan-Heeren (1987) *Afghanistan. Sozialer Wandel und Staat im 20. Jahrhundert* (Berlin).

Kleveman, Lutz (2002) *Der Kampf um das Heilige Feuer* (Berlin).

Medico International (2002) *circular 1*, pp. 8–11.

Roy, Olivier (1985) *L'Afghanistan. Islam et modernité politique* (Paris) [Persian version: Sarweghad Moghadam. Maschhad 1990].

Sigrist, Christian (1986) 'Der lange afghanische Krieg', *Das Argument*, Vol. 28, No. 157, pp. 378–90.

7
Nation-building by Occupation? – The Case of Iraq

Jochen Hippler

Iraq is one of the large number of multiethnic countries in the Third World whose borders were drawn by former colonial powers. After World War I, France and England shared a large part of the bankrupt estate of the Ottoman Empire and created the countries of Syria, Lebanon, Palestine, Transjordan and Iraq – with the latter awarded to England and officially administered as a trust territory of the League of Nations at that time. Its population was and remains heterogeneous, with over 70 per cent Arab and around one quarter Kurdish, plus smaller minorities, the largest of which is the Turkmen community. However, these groups are not homogeneous, either, with Sunni and Shiite Arabs opposing each other then as now, in addition to other Arab groups of lesser significance (for example the 'Marsh Arabs' in the south-east, with urban–rural differences and tribal structures also playing a role).

The Kurds, too, are not a unified entity: in the northern autonomy zone (established after the 1991 Gulf War), a war broke out between the two most important parties in the mid 1990s, which led to the emergence of two small Kurdish quasi-states which were not officially recognised. Up to 800,000 Kurds living in Baghdad are mostly of the Shiite faith, whereas those living in the main Kurdish area are mainly Sunnis. The political structures of Iraq have been weak since the founding of the state and initially even anachronistic: governed by Arab Sunnis whose power was supported by big land-owners and other power elites. Even the Iraqi king once remarked that his country was actually ungovernable. Faisal I stated the following in a confidential memorandum in 1933:

> (T)here is still – and I say this with a heart full of sorrow – no Iraqi people but unimaginable masses of human beings, devoid of any patriotic idea, imbued with religious traditions and absurdities, connected by no common

tie, giving ear to evil, prone to anarchy, and perpetually ready to rise against any government whatever. (Batatu 1982:25)

The years from 1958 to 1968 were a period of great instability, with the revolution followed by a decade of coups and countercoups and the first wave of Kurdish rebellions. Iraq had not been a 'nation' up to that time but, rather, a combination of heterogeneous social and ethnoreligious subsystems held together in a makeshift manner by an inadequately established state apparatus.

Following an initial, bloody and swiftly unsuccessful coup in 1963, the Arab-nationalist Baath party seized power in 1968 and did not relinquish it again until the Iraq War in 2003. Its extremely brutal dictatorship – Saddam Hussein formally took power in 1979 – represented an equally unscrupulous and ambitious attempt at nation-building. The country's previous instability was ended violently and through the greatly increased oil revenues of the 1970s and its multiethnic reality was to be compulsorily homogenised and Arabised. The infrastructure was modernised and partly developed in an exemplary manner with oil money, the previously weak state machinery was converted into an all-dominating power apparatus and the country was armed to an unprecedented level. Iraq laid claim to the role of leader in the Arab camp. A high-ranking representative of the regime told the author in 1991: 'We are happy to sacrifice one or two generations of Iraqis to make Iraq a great and powerful country.'

The war against Iran (1980–88) and the conquest of Kuwait were part of this context: the rival Iran was to be quickly defeated and eliminated as a competitor at a time of weakness (following the Islamic revolution) and, if possible, the oil-rich province of Khuzistan (with its Arab minority) snatched away from it. The conquest of Kuwait would not only have provided Iraq with further, substantial oil fields, its war-related foreign debts would likewise have been drastically reduced, with the country also acquiring an efficient port on the Persian Gulf. In both cases, however, these calculations of power politics came to nothing: although the war against Iran was won after severe setbacks and great effort, the country had been extremely weakened by heavy losses of people and infrastructure and through its war-related debts. The Gulf War defeat (1991) at the hands of a broad-based coalition led by the US, together with the subsequent international sanctions which lasted up to the Iraq War of 2003, ruined the country completely. A prosperous oil-producing country of the late 1970s had, before the turn of the millennium, been turned into a large slum with just a few small islands of affluence. The original recipe conceived by the Baath dictatorship of achieving stability through a combination of social, economic and infrastructure benefactions accompanied by brutal repression, of making Iraq a strong state and an international power player and of generally managing a successful Arab nation-building project had failed by the 1990s. From the combination of money and repression, only the latter was left to save the regime. One result of this development was that Iraqi society (with the exception of the Kurdish autonomous region in the north dealt with below) suffocated politically: all political work outside the dictatorship died or was pushed into exile and the cohesion of Iraqi society was hugely weakened. The different elements of society were held together virtually by the dictatorship alone, while all other political mechanisms of integration and articulation were repressed or smashed.

KURDISH AUTONOMY ENDEAVOURS

The Baathist nation-building project in Iraq clashed increasingly with a second undertaking which took shape in the 1960s and was close to being realised in the 1990s: the attempt to form Iraq into an Arab nation-state could only meet with opposition from the non-Arab minorities and especially from the Kurds. Kurdish resistance was first aimed predominantly at repelling outside tutelage and dominance by the central state, while an independent Kurdish national consciousness started to spread slowly in the course of the disputes. The dialectic of oppression and – also violent – resistance has led increasingly to the strengthening of a national Kurdish identity over the past few decades and, in political terms, to demands for autonomy or an independent state. This trend has, however, been repeatedly undermined by contradictions in the Kurdish camp, especially between the KDP and PUK parties (Kurdish Democratic Party and Patriotic Union Kurdistan respectively) as well as by overwhelming influence from the neighbouring countries (particularly Turkey and Iran), who have successfully played the two parties off against each other on repeated occasions and threatened military intervention (for the history of Iraqi Kurdistan, see Hippler 1990).

Kurdish sovereignty and nation-building have thus been thwarted by internal disunity, the government in Baghdad and the threats of neighbouring countries, while these factors have further strengthened the common identity and the population's aspiration to independence. When, however, a protection zone for the Kurds against Saddam Hussein was established in northern Iraq (in which around 60 per cent of the Iraqi Kurds were living) after the 1991 Gulf War, action was taken to form one and then two Kurdish protostates, which had their own governments, their own military, their own parliaments and their own currency up to 2003 and were, in reality, independent, even though not recognised under international law. This fact emphatically underlines the failure of the Baathist nation-building project, which was intended to make the entire country of Iraq a strong, Arab nation-state.

NECESSITY AND DIFFICULTY OF NATION-BUILDING

When the 2003 Iraq War brought down the dictatorship, all the mechanisms of social integration and the state apparatus collapsed with it. Unexpectedly and contrary to the experience in the 1991 Kurdish and Shiite revolt, the state apparatus disintegrated almost completely in the last few days of the war and just after. The vast majority of the military as well as the police, ministries and other authorities disappeared overnight, civil servants did not turn up for work any more and their offices were systematically looted and even burned down. At the end of the war, Iraq was a deeply traumatised and, outside the Kurdish autonomous zone, a stateless society with an extensively devastated infrastructure and economy, balancing on the extreme edge of chaos. The absence of political institutions, social integration mechanisms, functioning security authorities plus the countless instances of attacks and looting indicated that the war against Iraq had turned an all-powerful, repressive state into a failed state within an extremely short period of time.

Nation-building was not put on the agenda because Washington wanted or planned for it. Control of Iraq and 'regime change' were dominating political thinking in the US, not reshaping and integrating Iraqi society and rebuilding the state apparatus from scratch. Nation-building became crucial by default, not by design. Controlling and ruling a society of 25 million people, rebuilding the country and providing security and the required infrastructure, plus preparing it for some kind of Iraqi self-rule could all not be achieved without functioning state structures and related political mechanisms. And it all required systematic and effective ways to stop social fragmentation.

The starting position for a new attempt at nation-building proved to be very difficult after the war. The group of Sunni Arabs that had dominated the country up to the war (or a section of that part of the population) could only fear that they would lose most of their influence. This group had been oppressed to a lesser degree by the dictatorship, with most of the cadres and supporters recruited from it, and it was its members that derived the most benefit from the rule of Saddam Hussein in political and economic terms. With such a privileged position ruled out for the future, dissatisfaction with the new order was greatest and most immediate among this group. At the same time, the Sunni Arabs (or Arab Sunnis, depending on their own definition of themselves) did not have a leadership capable of action or any political organisations to speak of. This group of the population was fragmented, without leadership and politically almost impotent, which intensified the feeling of helplessness even further.

The situation was different among the Shiites. Despite their majority among the population, they had remained extensively excluded from power under Saddam (and in the preceding decades) and had – like the Kurds – suffered particularly under the brutality of the dictatorship. Now they could reckon with occupying an overall dominant position by putting up a united front vis-à-vis the other groups. The initial position of the Shiite Arabs (or Arab Shiites; leaving the special role of the Shiite Kurds in the greater Baghdad region out of consideration here) was characterised by the fact that, although their political organisations had been hit heavily and severely repressed by the dictatorship, their religiously inspired parties still existed in exile (and underground to a lesser degree). This means that they had an important political edge after the fall of the dictatorship, with quick and easy access to efficient political structures, money and their own armed militias on their return from Iran.

In contrast, the secular wing of Shiite Arabs was (despite strong potential) extensively disorganised and virtually incapable of political action. The previously significant Communist Party, which had been brutally smashed by Saddam, attempted to reorganise but lacked the financial resources and foreign support that the religious Shiite parties had at their disposal. For this reason, the politics of the Shiite Arabs were structured in a distinctly religious way despite their considerable secular instincts. There was therefore huge rivalry in the religious sector between the parties and currents, as well as between the distinct

Iranian influences and the existence of an 'Iraqi' interpretation of the Shia.

For the Kurdish population, especially in the Kurdish autonomous zone, the situation was fundamentally different to that in the rest of the country. The Kurds still had functioning political structures (the two parties and their protostate government authorities) and an extensively intact infrastructure, which had been developed over the period since 1991. Although a reorganisation of the political landscape in Iraqi Kurdistan can be expected in the medium term owing to the considerable and, since the fall of the Saddam dictatorship, constantly growing dissatisfaction of large sections of the population as a result of corruption, nepotism and the dictatorial behaviour of the two parties, it is not yet clear whether this will give rise to a 'third force' of younger, more modern forces or to any fundamental reform of the KDP and PUK. However, the stability and capacity for political action of the Kurdish autonomous region have remained at a high level despite this factor of uncertainty, especially compared with the remainder of the country. Nonetheless, there is a huge leaning among the Kurdish population and its parties in favour of independence from Iraq, though this is not demanded publicly for pragmatic reasons.

Kurdish policy therefore presses strongly for the federalisation of Iraq and actual Kurdish autonomy as minimum conditions for remaining in Iraq, though this could then be extended to sovereignty should the course of events prove unsatisfactory. At the same time, there are strong tendencies towards integrating the Kurdish areas outside the old autonomous zone into the Kurdish sphere of control as well as making the important oil city of Kirkuk and the area around Mosul Kurdish (again), something which harbours considerable potential for conflict vis-à-vis the Arab and Turkmen sections of the population.

However, an interethnic civil war is unlikely in the foreseeable future despite this constellation. Although occasional ethnic or interconfessional acts of violence can hardly be prevented at the local level, for example in the regions in and around Mosul and Kirkuk, this is not expected to spread over a large area for the time being. In particular, a new Kurdish–Arab war is not on the agenda, in spite of the potential for conflict that exists locally – the Kurdish side has no interest, anyway, while the Sunni and Shiite Arabs would not be in a position to pursue this line in the foreseeable future; in addition, most Shiites would find such an idea absurd. The relationship between the

Arab Shiites and the Kurds is more one of reserve, not hostility, with an informal coalition of the secular Kurds and the religious Shiite parties against the Sunnis even forming after the fall of the dictatorship. This Kurdish–Shiite link was weakened considerably in 2004, first because of the negotiation process in regard to a provisional constitution, and because of the military escalation in both Arab Sunni and Shiite areas in the spring of 2004. Still, if any larger-scale violence were to occur in the future, this would presumably be most likely directed against the occupation or take place within the Shiite population in the course of a struggle for political supremacy.

Seen against this background, nation-building is an extremely complex and difficult undertaking. The main political problems are the tendency of the only stable part of the country (the Kurdish autonomous zone) to break away from the state, the political paralysis and fragmentation of the Sunni Arabs as the traditional political elite, as well as the conflictive and religiously distorted political structure among the Arab Shiites. Added to this are the serious weaknesses of social and political integration mechanisms and the disastrous situation in the economic, social, security and infrastructure domains, which are giving rise to understandable dissatisfaction and considerable potential for conflict.

WASHINGTON'S POSTWAR PLANNING

Postwar planning began in August 2002 when a member of the National Security Council was instructed to recruit the appropriate competent specialists (*Washington Post* 2003a). The US State Department played a key role in the planning. However, on 20 January 2003, only weeks before the start of the war, President Bush decided that the Defense Department should be responsible for postwar planning.

> The State Department and other agencies spent many months and millions of dollars drafting strategies on issues ranging from a post-war legal code to oil policy. But after President Bush granted authority over reconstruction to the Pentagon, the Defense Department all but ignored State and its working groups. And once Baghdad fell, the military held its post-war team out of Iraq for nearly two weeks for security reasons, and then did not provide such basics as telephones, vehicles and interpreters for the understaffed operation to run a traumatized country of 24 million. (*Washington Post* 2003a)

The Pentagon's planning was carried out using limited personnel resources and over a comparatively short period; it was conducted by an Office of Special Plans, which worked so discretely that even Jay Garner, who had been appointed in January 2003 as the future civil administrator, also with responsibility for postwar planning, only learnt of its existence some weeks later. All the same, it was this office that stipulated the guidelines.

> Garner worked closely with Rumsfeld and Feith and met about once a week with national security adviser Condoleezza Rice. Only seven weeks before the war began, Garner's staff members could be counted on one hand, but he eventually assembled a staff that drew from a number of agencies. ... By March, after Garner arrived at a staging site in Kuwait, members of his own team believed that the administration had poorly prepared both Iraqis and Americans for what was to come. One U.S. official recalled, 'My uniformed friends kept telling me, "We're not ready. We're going into the beast's mouth."' (*Washington Post* 2003a)

The postwar planning was not only characterised by bureaucratic struggles, lack of personnel and improvisation; it was also based on misjudgements. It was assumed, for example, that the Iraqi population would enthusiastically welcome the US troops 'with flowers'. This is also why Garner told his staff that they should make themselves superfluous in Iraq 'within 90 days' (*Washington Post* 2003b). The passiveness and lack of preparation on the part of the occupying authorities contributed to many pressing tasks not being dealt with at all or only very unsatisfactorily. The rapid replacement of Jay Garner by Paul Bremer was evidence of this failure.

US OCCUPATION POLICY AND NATION-BUILDING

The US occupation policy was, especially in the first few months, characterised less by targeted planning than by improvisation and trial and error. The Pentagon had expected to be able to take over and use the effective Iraqi state apparatus (including its police force) more or less intact. Nation-building was not a declared objective of the occupying authorities and, for this reason, they were hardly prepared for it. The US authorities were geared up, in particular, to assume control, combat humanitarian crises (hunger, refugees) and hand over formal governmental authority (not necessary real power) to a new Iraqi government, the core of which was to be flown in from exile.

In this context, the Pentagon felt – in open conflict with the State Department and the CIA – that the prime choice for leader should be Ahmed Chalabi, who had close personal contacts with Vice-President Cheney, Secretary of Defense Rumsfeld and others. The idea of preserving the Iraqi state apparatus and simply providing it with a new, handpicked leadership quickly proved unrealistic, however: the authorities broke up virtually overnight, the police stayed at home, and Chalabi met with very strong disapproval from the Iraqi population. After the prompt handover of power to a group of acceptable exiles had failed and the state apparatus hardly existed any more, the task of state- and nation-building arose of its own accord. A functioning state system was indispensable for tackling the practical problems of a society of 24 million inhabitants, not least of all in order to control the population and ensure security. In addition, the uncertain situation within and between the different groups of the population necessitated political integration mechanisms that first had to be created.

These tasks were made substantially more difficult by the fact that living conditions in most of the country (with the exception of the Kurdish autonomous zone) were deteriorating severely under the occupying regime: the security situation immediately became dramatically worse, as the wave of looting in many towns and cities clearly illustrated. The US troops were playing an extremely dubious role in this context: in many cases, they refused, despite emphatic requests, to protect even hospitals or the national museum from looters while, in other instances, eye-witnesses reported that they actually encouraged looting. The German Embassy in Baghdad, for example, was first looted after a US tank had flattened the gate and US soldiers encouraged the perpetrators.[1]

One reason for the initially chaotic security situation was that the US had practically no military police at its disposal when the war in Iraq ended, which had particularly dramatic consequences in view of the ensuing looting. After the war, the US authorities in Iraq were, in particular, to

- ensure security for their own personnel and the Iraqi population;
- restore normal living conditions through reconstructing the technical, social and economic infrastructure, especially

electricity and water supplies plus medical and social facilities;

- safeguard the social cohesion of Iraq and prevent tendencies towards disintegration; and
- establish a new political system to which political power could be transferred in the medium term without harming their own interests.

The first two tasks, the fulfilment of which was necessary in order to stabilise the country in the short term, to legitimise the occupation and to create conditions for control and nation-building, were tackled with alarming cluelessness. The US authorities could only establish the security of their own troops to a very limited extent, with more US soldiers killed in attacks by the summer of 2003 than during the actual war, and the situation further deteriorating since the spring of 2004. More significant in political terms, however, was the fact that the Iraqi civil population was even far less secure than the occupiers, with spontaneous and organised violent crime, political intimidation and force, plus general lawlessness developing into a daily threat for the population at large. For this reason, the criticism was frequently levelled that: 'The US troops are very interested in security – but only in their own, not ours.'[2]

Reestablishment of the civil infrastructure also proceeded at an astonishingly sluggish pace and without success in the first few months, with the electricity supply in Baghdad functioning only seven to eight hours a day and just two to four hours a day in cities like Mosul, according to the complaints of local residents. Even in March of 2004 Baghdad residents still complained of the power supply being cut four times a day for two to three hours each time. Without electricity, other public services are also restricted; no electricity means no water supply because the pumps cannot work. In intense heat (up to 60°C in summer 2003), restrictions of this nature had an especially grave and direct impact on the health situation – especially under conditions of makeshift medical care services. One high-ranking US official commented on the problem as follows at the beginning of July 2003:

'Power is the central issue,' a senior U.S. official here said. 'Without it, you don't have security. You don't have an economy. You don't have trust in what we're doing. What you do have is more anger, more frustration, more violence. We're not going to solve anything here until we first find a way to get more electricity to the people.' (*Washington Post* 2003c).

Criticism of the severe shortcomings in the areas of security and infrastructure was already widespread in the summer of 2003 and increasing well into in 2004 (outside the better-organised Kurdish autonomous zone), with differences principally evident in terms of how they were assessed politically: one part of the population pleaded for patience, while others became increasingly louder in their demand for the withdrawal of the occupying troops and for responsibility to be handed over to Iraqi bodies.

Serious problems also soon surfaced in relation to the introduction of new social and political integration mechanisms and state-building. For example, a further 15,000–30,000 civil servants were, contrary to the original plans, dismissed by the US civil administrator, Paul Bremer, on political grounds (because of actual or alleged links with the dictatorship) (*Washington Post* 2003c) while, at the same time, high-ranking officials of the Saddam regime were promoted to key positions, such as the new governor of Mosul, an incriminated army general. Local elections were prepared in numerous towns and cities but then stopped by Bremer at the last minute because an acceptable election outcome could not be guaranteed (*New York Times* 2003a; *Washington Post* 2003d).

The impression thus emerged that, although the US spoke of democracy, it did not want to permit it unless it had complete control of the process. Where Jay Garner had already promised at the beginning of May 2003 that there would be a new Iraqi government the same month (*New York Times* 2003b), this was no longer the case just a few weeks later. This situation was underlined by the formation and handling of the 'Provisional Governing Council' and the subsequently appointed ministers: contrary to the original promises, the Council was not chosen by a large 'National Assembly' of Iraqis; it was determined exclusively by the occupying power (*New York Times* 2003b). The Council was not given responsibility for government, rather only advisory functions. Despite the uncertain security situation, the US troops even declined to provide the Governing Council the 100 rifles requested for their bodyguards (four for each member), saying that these could be acquired elsewhere. (They were eventually obtained from the Kurdish military.) The 'Governing Council' was not allowed any influence on practical policy-making, e.g. in the domains of security, infrastructure or the awarding of contracts to companies for reconstruction. It was predominantly a PR exercise designed to symbolise the hope for a subsequent takeover of power by the Iraqis. The reality was different. US civil administrator Bremer stated with gratifying clarity: 'As long as we are here, we are the occupying power. It's an ugly word, but it's the truth' (*Washington Post* 2003e).

The Iraqi population reacted to the situation of occupation in different ways. The vast majority of the Kurds had welcomed Washington's war against Iraq because it was seen as the only way of bringing down the dictatorship. The US troops were and continue to be accepted and are being asked to stay permanently because only they can guarantee security against the threats coming from Turkey and Iran, who are both extremely suspicious of Kurdish autonomy or even independence in Iraq for internal political reasons. US presence is also seen as an insurance against attempts by subsequent governments in Baghdad to regain control of Kurdistan, even though there is widespread distrust of Washington. The Arab Sunni regions have the least hopes of anything positive emerging from the US occupation, and have hardly anything to gain from it. It was no surprise that military resistance to the occupation started in Arab Sunni areas, with a broad-based insurgency in Falluja becoming a symbol of this resistance. The heavy-handed tactics of the US occupation forces greatly contributed to this resistance. Among the Shiite Arab population there has been a distinct ambivalence in regard to US occupation. On the one hand, Shiites were relieved and thankful that Saddam Hussein had been toppled. At the same time, however, they were very suspicious of US policy, accusing it of striving for supremacy in the region and control of the Iraqi oil deposits. Many Shiites already felt cheated by the US by summer and autumn 2003: promises were not kept and living conditions were difficult to endure. Among Arab Sunnis and Shiites, such growing antipathies sometimes gave rise to absurd conspiracy theories, for example speculation on whether the US was possibly responsible for the bomb attacks on the UN Headquarters and the Imam Ali mosque in Najaf.

At the time of writing, the political mood in Iraq had deteriorated for two reasons. First, the population's patience diminished with the continuing situation of lawlessness and disastrous living conditions, thus lessening the political credit of the US; second, the unresolved security problem (and the US response to it) had severe political consequences: the numerous attacks on US soldiers forced the occupying troops to distance themselves more from the population and be suspicious of Iraqi civilians, acting towards them in a security-centred manner. The desired image of liberators had increasingly turned into one of mere occupiers, at least in the Arab territories.

When violence and resistance to the occupation in the Sunni triangle became complemented by similar practices in the Shiite areas, Washington's position became politically fragile. Arab Sunni violence was a nuisance, but could have been kept under control over time, if it would have been occurring in a context of a peaceful north and south, that is Kurdish and Shiite areas. But with parts of the Iraqi Shiites joining military resistance to the occupation, it increasingly became questionable whether occupation was feasible in the long run. Shiite insurgency was not a general uprising of Iraqi Shiites, but organised by one Shiite group which was in the danger of being politically marginalised, Muqtada Sadr's 'Mahdi Army'. The majority of Shiites and of Shiite parties still did not feel the need for violent resistance when the fighting began. For them, peaceful struggle still seemed the most attractive option, since power would necessarily fall to the Shiites in a framework of elections because of their constituting the majority of the population. But because of the increasing resentment of US occupation the Shiite clergy and parties like Dawa and SCIRI were put in an awkward situation: being hostile towards Muqtada Sadr's movement and their tactics, but not being able to confront them out of fear of appearing as collaborators in the occupation. As a result Muqtada's support in the Shiite community increased.

The fragile situation of the occupation put the question of transfer of power to an Iraqi government at the top of the agenda. The need for transfer increased with the worsening of the security situation, with the loss of acceptance and of prestige of the US occupation, while the chances of a peaceful, orderly and well-designed transfer weakened. Instability, insecurity, together with the weakening of Washington's political strength in Iraq and its lack of planning made the handover of power more and more difficult, while delaying it would have fanned resistance to the occupation even more. Nation-building and state-building became more urgent then ever, but the US capacity to control and shape it had diminished. US tactics now rediscovered the United Nations as an actor in Iraq. Lakhdar Brahimi, the UN representative to Iraq was declared to have a free hand in drawing up a plan for the transition of power and selecting suitable personnel. In the meantime it became more obvious that internal dynamics had started a realignment of political forces in Iraq: even US-appointed and pro-US politicians and parties had to distance themselves more and more from Washington in order not to appear as mere US puppets and lose any credibility inside Iraq. As a result, neither the UN nor the US could force their candidates for the jobs of prime minister and president of the future Iraqi government. The US-appointed Governing Council prevailed in selecting the key positions, thereby demonstrating a weakening foreign influence and its intention to secure jobs for most of its members despite their lack of public support. The selection process of the new government constituted a double minicoup of artificially selected politicians with a limited public base against their foreign masters and the aspirations of their own population. In the context of both Iraqi nation-building and stabilisation, the transfer of power from the US occupation authorities to an Iraqi government on 30 June 2004 was an ambiguous affair: on the one hand it was the only way forward, since further occupation would become increasingly untenable. On the other hand, it was still less than clear whether the US designs for a power transfer could work: Washington started from the assumption that the new, 'sovereign' government should neither have command over its own military forces (much less a say in regard to continuing US military operations), nor the right to change or pass any laws. This would have installed a government without the ability to actually govern. Such a design would easily have turned the Iraqi population against such a government, since it would have been perceived merely as a US-inspired PR exercise to shift the blame for its policies to Iraqis, without giving them actual power. In the process of negotiating a new UN resolution to legitimise the new setup in Iraq, Washington had to compromise and the role of the new government got strengthened. But it sill is too early to judge whether the new design has a chance to succeed.

NATION-BUILDING THROUGH WAR AND OCCUPATION?

The US's nation-building experiment in Iraq was in a state of crisis after six months, and bordering on failure after a year. Too little and very slow headway was being made with the reconstruction and reestablishment of the most necessary infrastructure, the security situation remained strained and was deteriorating even further. The handover of power to an Iraqi government was a complex and poorly planned affair with an uncertain outcome. The newly created bodies of Iraqi politics – especially the Provisional Governing Council and the ministers appointed by it – had few if any administrative functions and were being kept away from real power by the US occupation. The US troops on the ground principally focused their concentration, for obvious reasons, on the military security of their own units, which, however, repeatedly lead to unintended victims among the civil population or even Iraqi policemen and increased the scepticism shown towards the occupiers. The scandal over torture of Iraqi prisoners in US-run prisons did not make things better. To ensure a successful policy, the US urgently needed an 'Iraqisation' of the security system which did not work satisfactory. However, it also wanted to keep a firm grip on this 'Iraqisation', which gave the new institutions a colonial flavour and lead to allegations of collaboration by their staff. This will undermine the legitimacy of the occupation over the long term.

The fact that Washington never developed any recognisable concept for Iraqi nation-building and was instead intent on resolutely muddling its way through is another significant problem. This exists for two reasons: first, because any role by the military in nation-building continues to be rejected (although this stance is being eased in view of the actual requirements) and, second, because there is an almost irresolvable conflict of objectives between the requirements of military occupation and imperial control on the one hand and those of a transfer of power to civilian protagonists and medium-term nation-building on the other hand.

But the main stumbling block for an orderly transfer of power was the problem that the occupation forces had very few attractive options as regards to whom to transfer power. Many of the pro-US actors were hardly more than artificial creations of the US itself, and thereby tainted as tools of the occupation with little backing inside Iraq. The Kurdish parties did have political support in the Kurdish areas, but none further south, and they were only tactically supporting Iraqi nation-building because their main interest was building their own state, outside or only loosely connected to Iraq. And the religiously inspired Shiite parties were deeply distrusted by Washington and were difficult to instrumentalise by the United States because of their own agendas.

If we apply the three main criteria for successful nation-building, that is state-building, integrating society, and an integrative ideology (see Hippler, Chapter 14, this volume), the results of US-led policies in Iraq in 2004/05 are less than impressive. One, Washington was mostly responsible for turning an all-powerful and oppressive state into a failed state. Two, it was neither conceptionally nor materially prepared to deal with this situation it had created. Three, the slow speed and incompetence in rebuilding Iraqi infrastructure and the heavy-handed military occupation taxed the patience of the population with foreign troops and policies and dramatically reduced US credibility. The result was deep mistrust against the occupation in the Arab areas and its nation-building attempts. Four, internal conditions for nation-building in Iraq are highly complex, since it requires a careful rebalancing of ethnic and religious parts of the population, without 'ethnicising' the political process. The Arab Shiite groups are expecting the lion's share of power, which will be difficult for many Sunni Arabs, given their tradition of dominance. And the Kurdish parties can only be bribed to remain inside Iraq with a highly disproportional share of power in Baghdad, which will trigger resentment among Arabs.

The US occupation experiment may have legally ended in July 2004, but for most practical purposes it will continue as long as US troops militarily dominate Iraq. It has not yet failed, but it is in dangerous waters. Success or failure cannot be reliably predicted as yet, but both are possible scenarios. However, in 2004 US-dominated nation-building for Iraq was on its way down. The Kurdish parties were discreetly pushing for their own version of nation-building, as were the Shiite parties, with the US forces increasingly less able to unilaterally shape Iraqi politics.

NOTES

1. Accounts related to the author by witnesses, Baghdad, August 2003.
2. Statements made to the author in Baghdad, Karbala and Najaf, August 2003 and March 2004.

REFERENCES

Batatu, Hanna (1982) *The Old Social Classes and the Revolutionary Movements of Iraq* (Princeton, NJ).

Hippler, Jochen (1990) 'Kurdistan – Ein ungelöstes Problem im Mittleren Osten', *Vereinte Nationen*, December, pp. 202–5.

New York Times (2003a) 'Iraqis were Set to Vote, but U.S. Wielded a Veto', *New York Times*, Internet edition of 19 June.

New York Times (2003b) 'In Reversal, Plan for Iraq Self-Rule Has Been Put off', *New York Times*, Internet edition of 17 May.

Washington Post (2003a) 'Wolfowitz Concedes Iraq Errors', *Washington Post*, 24 July, p. A01.

Washington Post (2003b) 'Reconstruction Planners Worry, Wait and Re-Evaluate', *Washington Post*, 2 April, p. A01.

Washington Post (2003c) 'Blackout Return, Deepening Iraq's Dark Days', *Washington Post*, 3 July, S. A01.

Washington Post (2003d) 'Plan to Secure Post-war Iraq Faulted', *Washington Post*, 19 May, p. A01.

Washington Post (2003e) 'Occupation Forces Halt Elections throughout Iraq', *Washington Post*, 28 June, p. A20.

8

Between Self-determination and Multiethnicity – International Actors and Nation-building in Bosnia and Kosovo

Dušan Reljić

The outcome of nation-building in the conflict regions of the West Balkans over the past 15 years has – since the beginning of the disintegration of Yugoslavia – been determined exclusively by the West and principally by the US. In the end, the external effect has left little sign of the initial intentions of the local political leaders whose nationalistic politics had led to ethnopolitical conflicts and war. The two most important 'national projects' occupying the political scene in place of the Titoist model of multiethnic 'brotherhood and unity' during the period of disintegration of the former Yugoslavia, that is the dreams of a 'Greater Serbia' and 'Greater Croatia', failed, for example, as a result of outside intervention. Other nationalist movements have also found it impossible to realise their maximum objectives, at least up to now: the Muslims have not risen to become the dominant titular nation in Bosnia and Herzegovina, an Albanian-dominated Kosovo still has to overcome some uncertain ground before attaining actual independence, and whether the emergence of a 'Greater Albania' will one day find its way onto the international agenda is something that is still written in the stars.

At the same time, external state actors intervening in the conflicts in various forms were also transformed by the armed clashes that took place in the former Yugoslavia between 1991 and 1999. It was, for example, Germany which, after a half-century of 'abstinence' following World War II, activated the military component of foreign policy by taking part in armed interventions in the former Yugoslavia. Russia proved to be a 'paper tiger' – unable to project power outside the boundaries of the former Soviet Union. Moscow has, in the meantime, completely withdrawn its peace-keeping troops from Bosnia and Kosovo.

Only the US has so far been able to chalk up any distinct successes in the fragmented Yugoslavia, with Washington strengthening both its claim to leadership within NATO and its 'credibility' as a global decision-maker by leading the West's military interventions on the territory of the former Yugoslavia and then also stipulating the essential terms of the peace settlements in Croatia and Bosnia as well as for Kosovo. A *pax Americana* has come about on the territory of the former Yugoslavia. The European Union, although it wanted to play a leading role – especially at the beginning of the armed phase of the conflict in 1991 – has not been able to assert its ideas. With the US having turned its attention towards the 'war on terror', the EU is now acting increasingly in this region with a type of general power of attorney granted by Washington.[1]

Before examining the performance of the international actors in greater detail, let us first take a look at the current situation. How stable is this post-Yugoslavian peace framework imposed 'from outside'? How do things look in the region with regard to democracy and socioeconomic progress as central areas of the nation-building process?

INTERIM APPRAISAL OF THE FORMER YUGOSLAVIA

The three wars waged on the territory of the former Yugoslavia since 1991 in Slovenia, Croatia and Bosnia, together with the 1998 rebellion in Kosovo and the NATO attacks on Bosnian Serbs in 1995 and then on Serbia itself in 1999, cost tens of thousands of lives and caused deep divisions between the ethnic groups in the region. It took just one decade for the territory of the former Yugoslavia to fragment – a state which had previously endured for seven decades, even enjoying a certain degree of importance in world politics as the most powerful country in its region.

The interventions by the West have so far mainly served to stop the bloodshed and protected the region against any further spread of the chaotic conditions that broke out as a result of the dissolution of state structures. However, no workable regional state order with effective internal and external security structures has yet developed, even though no other region in the world has had so many influential external state and non-state actors present for over a decade, all trying to promote or directly establish stability and democracy.

The situation is worst in Kosovo, where the external intervention has been greatest; even four years after the arrival of the NATO-led international peace-keeping troops, there is still no elementary security for members of minority groups. Consequently, there are ever fewer people from minorities living there – of the 230,000 Serbs and other non-Albanians who fled to safety before the international peace-keeping troops arrived only a small number have returned to Kosovo. Even the majority ethnic group is threatened by terror, corruption and organised crime. The international protectorate itself is increasingly proving to be the opposite of a model for democracy. In the words of the Council of Europe's human rights envoy, Alvaro Gil-Robles, commenting on the state of the UN administration at the end of 2002: '... it is clear that the very structure of the international administration as well as certain powers retained by its various branches, substantially deviate from international human rights norms and the accepted principles of the rule of law' (Gil-Robles 2002:4).

A former justice expert of the international administration in Bosnia-Herzegovina and Kosovo, Dr Axel Schwarz, spoke in his analysis of the power structures of the UN administration in Kosovo (UNMIK) of a 'return of absolutism' (Schwarz 2002:527).

Nor do the social, political and economic structures in Bosnia-Herzegovina in any way fulfil the expectations and needs there, and this despite huge financial allocations and the long-term work of a large number of Western aid organisations. The UN protectorate administrator, Paddy Ashdown, and his predecessors have taken major decisions by decree, from the 'ethically neutral design' of the new national flag to the removal of high-ranking democratically elected politicians in Bosnia-Herzegovina. However, the political institutions created by the West have not produced the desired results. As an independent state, Bosnia-Herzegovina depends on the presence of the West. Political heteronomy and outside military presence will undoubtedly continue for a number of years.

The lack of internal consolidation in the former conflict regions of ex-Yugoslavia goes hand in hand with uncertain prospects in relation to linking these entities to European integration processes in the near future. While substantial progress has been made on the continent over the last decade in the area of political and economic integration, particularly by way of the recent accession of a number of Central and Eastern European countries to the EU, the new states of Southeast Europe (with the exception of Slovenia) remain in an unstable state with uncertain prospects. Further national fragmentation (e.g. disintegration of the entity of 'Serbia and Montenegro' or the secession of Kosovo) is at least just as likely as the forging of closer links to the EU in the short term.

Since the beginning of Western interventions in the former Yugoslavia, which also signalled the start of the emergence of new nation-states in the region, the number of new political subjects claiming independent status under international law in that region has constantly increased. There are now nine political entities on the territory of the former Socialist Federal Republic of Yugoslavia – or even more depending on whether Serbia and Montenegro are referred to as one or two states, Kosovo is still counted as part of Serbia, Bosnia is regarded as being divided in two or three and the predominantly Albanian-settled regions of west Macedonia are deemed already detached from Skopje or, indeed, indications of the outlines of an all-Albanian state are recognised. What all of the post-Yugoslavian autonomies that actually do exist have in common is their severely restricted sovereignty: there are UN protectorates in Bosnia and Herzegovina as well as Kosovo, while Macedonia and Montenegro are extensively dependent on the West, and Serbia, Croatia and Slovenia need the goodwill of Western centres of power in every respect. As long as the new states remain so weak, both in terms of their dependence on centres of power in the West and their limited ability to perform internal state functions, it will hardly be possible to make headway in establishing regional stability and democratisation or furthering economic and social development.

In economic and social terms, the region has fallen apart since the demise of the former Yugoslavia, setting it back several decades. Only Slovenia has been able to regain the economic power that it enjoyed in 1989; Serbia, the most populous former constituent republic of Yugoslavia now generates just half the gross national product of that year, when the violent process of disintegration was imminent. In Macedonia and Bosnia-Herzegovina, the statistics are even more disastrous. Seven new currencies (including the euro in Montenegro) have emerged to replace the Yugoslav dinar. On the important former pan-Yugoslavian north–south highway (E70), the fastest link between Central Europe and the Near East, there are now customs checks every 300–400 kilometres. The change in the region has so far taken the form of a general step backwards in economic and social terms compared with the period prior to 1991. Deindustrialisation, unemployment and depopulation are only a few of the disheartening processes that are destroying social cohesion in the region over the long term, thus ruining the foundations for nation-building.

STRUCTURE AND JUSTIFICATION OF FRAGMENTATION

The beginning of the West's nation-building in Bosnia-Herzegovina, Kosovo and the other parts of the former Yugoslavia was undoubtedly marked by local ethnopolitical conflicts. They were an expression of failed modernisation and numerous other weaknesses in the political and economic development of the southern Slavic state since 1918. The nationalist outbursts that occurred in the former Yugoslavia in the late 1980s were inflamed even more by the change in world politics during the demise of the Soviet Union. The failure of the power elite – after the death of the absolute dictator for many years, Josip Broz Tito (1980), in what was already a fragmented state – to manage economic and political change as long as there was still stability in the international environment had disastrous consequences.

Virtually from the outset, however, it was no longer possible to speak of any local ownership in the political dynamics that developed during the course of the demise of Yugoslavia. The local actors only had prospects of success insofar as they were able to win the outside protecting powers over to their side. The primary concern of the national leaders was to gain recognition of their political claims and find powerful external allies against their opponents within Yugoslavia. In this way, the local political actors inevitably became clients of external protecting powers to an ever-greater extent. States of dependence developed which left the local partners little scope for action. The Croatian, Serbian and Muslim political leaders, for example, eventually signed the peace agreement for Bosnia-Herzegovina in Dayton in 1995, which did not meet the war objectives of any of the three sides. Four years later, an interim solution for Kosovo was set out in UN Resolution 1244. Neither the Albanian rebels nor the government in Belgrade were involved in this coming about. The real actors engaged in the ethnopolitical conflicts had only minor roles in the end game with hardly any other choice than to accept the will of the West – and, in particular, of the US.

In this context, the demand for self-determination is the central concept of nationalist politics. The 'death' of Yugoslavia in ethnopolitical conflicts and wars was brought about in the name of the nation, as the birth of the right to national self-determination. However, it was not the monoethnic creations (ethnically pure nations) longed for by the nationalistic obstetricians that arose from this bloody act of procreation.[2] In the end, most of the nationalist projects in the former Yugoslavia were thwarted by the intervention of outside powers. This occurred unexpectedly insofar as the external intervention in the initial phase (1989–92) was carried out primarily in the name of the people's right of self-determination. The support for the secession of Slovenia and Croatia was, especially in newly reunited Germany, justified in 1990 on the grounds of the paramount importance of the right of self-determination. The abandonment of the common, multiethnic state was deemed necessary to enable the individual southern Slavic nations to exercise their right of self-determination. The nationalist principle, condensed in the endeavour to establish one's identity between ethnic and political boundaries, was given priority. The ethnic pluralism in the constituent republics of Yugoslavia was to be taken account of by the states with the help of laws to protect the minorities. The fact was totally ignored in this respect that the 'new' minorities had previously lived in a common state for 70 years and now, overnight, had to become citizens of a state that was hostile to them, given that the 'national ideology' in the new states was generally based on stirring up rejection and hatred towards the 'other' nations (the new minorities). Nevertheless, the right to self-determination was – with the help of the West – interpreted as the right of nationalist movements to form nation-states in place of a multinational federation. This provided, in essence, support for the force- and war-oriented policy of the nationalist movements, into which the communist power institutions in the constituent republics of Yugoslavia had transformed themselves after the end of one-party rule.

In Germany, in particular, there was a widespread national-romantic view of the conflict situation. This was expressed in the axiomatic call that Germany, which had regained its unity on the basis of the right to self-determination, could on no account refuse support for Slovenia and Croatia, which were also demanding the right to self-determination. Federal Chancellor Helmut Kohl even spoke of a 'particularly intensive relationship between the Germans and the Croatians' which had 'very much to do with history' (Federal Press Office, 16.1.1992). The media had already printed an observation by the Soviet leader, Mikhail Gorbachev, according to which there existed 'as it were a genetic predisposition to friendship between the Russian and Serbian peoples'. In both cases, this gave expression to an effusively romantic view of the situation that bore no relation to the actual political developments, which were primarily concerned with questions regarding control over ethnically 'cleansed' territories.

A view of the Yugoslav conflict fixed solely on the right of self-determination of the peoples tended to overlook the fact that the political borders within Yugoslavia were, with few exceptions, not identical to ethnic borders, with this especially the case in Bosnia and Herzegovina. The right of self-determination of the peoples as a priority for intervention by the West came to an abrupt end the moment Bosnia and Herzegovina, the 'most Yugoslavian' of all the constituent republics by virtue of being almost completely multiethnic and having no titular nation, became embroiled in a three-way civil war in 1992/93.[3] The bloodshed was halted in 1995 by the military intervention, led by the US, against the Bosnian Serbs. A year earlier at meetings in Bonn and Washington, the Bosnians (Muslims) and Croats were forced into a joint federation under the most enormous political pressure. The results of the West's political and military intervention were transformed politically into the Dayton Peace Accord.

Washington and the Western allies declared their readiness from that point on to recognise a new ethnic entity – Republika Srpska – as a consideration for the willingness of the Bosnian Serbs to remain in Bosnia and Herzegovina within the framework of a decentralised state. This thwarted the plans of Croat and Serb nationalists to split up Bosnia and annex the captured areas to the 'motherland'. The Dayton Accord did, however, permit the Bosnian Serbs and Croats vaguely defined 'special relations' with Serbia and Croatia, through which the sovereignty of Bosnia-Herzegovina was partially set aside forthwith. With the dividing-up of this former constituent republic of Yugoslavia into cantons at the lowest structural level and the Muslim–Croat federation constituting the reformed state together with Republika Srpska, the creators of the Dayton Accord wanted to take account of the ethnopolitical division of Bosnia-Herzegovina, but leave the external borders unchanged – a plan equivalent to the proverbial squaring of the circle.

In the spring of 2003, the British historian, Timothy Garton Ash, wrote in relation to the problem of self-determination: 'As so often, we can only twist and turn helplessly when confronted with the subject of "self-determination"' (*Die Welt*, 31.03.2003). The occasion for this opinion was the refusal of the West to support the Kurds in Iraq and Turkey in their autonomy endeavours while, according to Ash, it was in the process of helping the Kosovo Albanians to gain independence from Serbia.

EXTERNAL NATION-BUILDING AS A STATE OF LIMBO

A number of constructs unprecedented under international law have emerged as a result of the West's nation-building endeavours in the former Yugoslavia. In view of the fact that, even eight years after the peace agreement reached in Dayton, the complex constitution in Bosnia-Herzegovina can only be maintained – as in Kosovo since 1999 – by a 'proconsul' in the name of the UN possessing all the power and also using it, the number of voices demanding that the Dayton Accord be revised is increasing. However, nobody dares to make any really serious move in this direction because the consequences for the fragile peace in the entire region could be incalculable. Furthermore, the attention of the US following the events of September 11, 2001 could well be focused squarely on the 'war on terror' for quite some time yet. Bosnia-Herzegovina thus remains an incomplete attempt to take hold again of the nationalist spirit which the West essentially encouraged by supporting the transformation of the Yugoslav constituent republics of Slovenia and Croatia into independent nation-states. The contemplation of multiethnicity has come too late.

In the case of Kosovo, the inconsistency of the West's action has been fully revealed. The military intervention led by the US ended the affiliation of the previously autonomous province to Serbia in practical terms in 1999 without, however, formally establishing any definite new situation under international law. At the same time, in no other part of the former Yugoslavia was ethnic homogenisation as far reaching as in Kosovo after the West's intervention: the Albanians are now extensively living among themselves, without any significant prospect of the non-Albanians that fled returning. Nevertheless, in the runup to the US attack on Iraq, the West's nation-building endeavours in Kosovo were often cited as an 'example of relative success' and something to be emulated in other failed states (Rice 2003:6). On the other hand, the example of Bosnia led the US Assistant Secretary of State, Paul D. Wolfowitz, to stress that it could be dangerous to hold democratic elections in Iraq straight away in order to simply prove that democracy was taking root there. According to the influential strategist, 'dangerously divisive leaders' could come to power (in an interview with the *New York Times*, 21.05.2003).

A further consequence of the ethnic homogenisation that occurred in Kosovo after 1999 is the emergence of an extended Albanian monoethnic region in the south west of the Balkan Peninsula which, in addition to the southern Serbian province, also covers western Macedonia and Albania. The political borders between four countries still remain. The West – and now, in particular, the EU – does not dare to address this inconsistency because there is a fear that any union of the Albanian nation would give rise to an uncontrollable domino effect for the rest of the region: how could the Croats and Serbs in Bosnia-Herzegovina then be stopped from demanding unification with their 'mother nations'? Would the state of Macedonia, held together through a great effort on the part of the EU and US, then promptly perish?

The 'Albanian question' awaits an answer, which, as expressed very sensitively in a recent report by the United States Institute of Peace, 'will almost surely require more extensive regional arrangements than exist today' (USIP 2002:4). The process of removing previous state structures in the region and establishing new political entities has evidently not been completed by any means. The outcome of the external military-political interventions that have taken place in the former Yugoslavia over the past decade is thus still open in many respects. At present, the Albanian pressure for secession in Kosovo and Macedonia is only restrained by huge threats from the West. In Montenegro, the faction of politicians striving for independence around Prime Minister Milo Đukanović has temporarily put its intentions on ice solely because of the West's disapproval. All in all, it has to be assumed that the transformation of the ethnopolitical conflicts in the region will continue to proceed in the future under considerable and decisive influence from outside.

THE EU AND US AS 'NATION-BUILDERS' IN THE BALKANS

Since 2001, the European Union has gradually taken over the initiative (and predominant responsibility) for the long-term pacification of the former Yugoslavia from the US. The West's nation-building activities in the former Yugoslavia are presently being carried out – in terms of the main features involved – as part of the EU's Common Foreign and Security Policy. The forced birth of Serbia and Montenegro in 2002/03 took place at the behest of the EU, personified by its foreign policy representative, Xavier Solana, who, on 14 March 2002, forced the top politicians in Belgrade and Podgorica to sign an agreement on the transformation of the Federal Republic of Yugoslavia into the entity of 'Serbia and Montenegro', with no more precise definition under constitutional law. (No surprise then when the new creation was promptly dubbed 'Solania'.) At the same time, the EU assumed central security responsibilities in Macedonia and Bosnia-Herzegovina. Together with the loans from the World Bank and the International Monetary Fund, the monies provided by the EU (for example via the reconstruction programme, CARDS, plus the European Agency for Reconstruction) are the most important source of finance for the Yugoslav succession states, which suffer from excessive debt, high foreign trade deficits and a lack of direct foreign investment.

Has the EU taken on too much in the former Yugoslavia financially and politically? Will its commitment as a 'nation-builder' in the region end in disgrace? There is strong endorsement for the independence of Kosovo both in the US Congress and in numerous Washington think-tanks. It is not clear to an important section of the political class in the US capital why war was waged against Serbia in 1999 if the Kosovo Albanians are, nevertheless, not constitutionally allowed to leave Serbia. The prevailing view among diplomats and political scientists in the EU, however, is that an independent Kosovo would form the nucleus of a Greater Albania. For this reason, Brussels is at pains to defer the question of the final status for Kosovo for as long as possible and on no account permit the separation of Montenegro so as to prevent the Albanian political leaders from using the independence of Montenegro as an opportunity for the secession of Kosovo. The EU places its faith in regional integration processes, which it is hoped will pacify the region of the former Yugoslavia to such an extent that accession to the EU would even be possible eventually. It is hoped that this will preclude any further fragmentation, which would most likely be accompanied by new armed conflicts. As a political instrument, the EU has established the so-called Stabilisation and Association Process (SAP). The SAP does not, however, comprise any guarantee for future membership of the EU. It is hoped that a stabilising effect will be brought about by the prospect of possible membership alone. In concrete terms, it is hoped to steer the political goals of the actors in Bosnia-Herzegovina, Kosovo and Montenegro towards the SAP, which also places great emphasis on regional cooperation, and away from self-determination in the sense of establishing their own monoethnic states.

This EU instrument does not appear to offer sufficient incentives at present, especially with regard to financial assistance or for boosting the economy and employment and gaining access to the international market. It is also evident that the EU strategists have developed the SAP under the assumption that they are dealing with developed nations and states. What we have in the West Balkans, however, are either weak states or state-type entities, like Kosovo, which first wish to attain clarification of their status before wanting or being able to enter into transnational unions.

It is therefore not surprising that the political leaders in Priština and Podgorica are still seeking support among politicians in the US who are favourably disposed towards them. These include important foreign-policy figures in the US Congress like Henry Hyde, Tomas Lantos, Joseph Biden and the Mayor of New York, Michael Bloomberg. The Kosovo Albanians fundamentally reject political negotiations with the Serbian side without US involvement. They are hoping that the US will exercise its authority again, as it did in 1995 in Croatia and Bosnia and in 1999 in Kosovo. Although the present US government has so far shown no indications of being prepared to go it alone, the differences of opinion in the political communities of the US and Western Europe with regard to Kosovo are huge. Over the long term, the advocates of a more strongly proactive Western policy on the matter of the final status of Kosovo could gain strength – especially if the impression were to be reinforced that the work of the UN administrators in Bosnia and Kosovo is fruitless. This possibility was pointed out by, among others, the Paris Institute for Security Studies – a body close to the EU – in March 2003 in a summary concerning the consequences of the impending reduction of the US military presence in the Balkans (Triantaphyllou 2003:2). There is the possibility of a conflict looming once again between the US and the EU, which could, in particular, cause severe harm to the delicate growth of the EU's Common Foreign and Security Policy.

The US had already actively torpedoed the efforts of the EU envoys to the former Yugoslavia once before, i.e. between 1991 and 1993, when the EU was attempting to find a political solution for the region. In the words of the US Secretary of State at the time, James Baker:

Some Europeans – certain that political and monetary union was coming and would create a European superpower – were headstrong about asserting a European defense identity in which America's role on the Continent was minimized. We had been fighting this for some time, and trying to get them to recognize that, even with a diminished Soviet threat, they still needed an engaged America. But our protestations were overlooked in an emotional rush for a unified Europe. The result was an undercurrent in Washington, often felt but seldom spoken, that it was time to make the Europeans step up to the plate and show that they could act as a unified power. Yugoslavia was as good a first test as any. (Baker 1995:637)

Not much has changed in this respect since then: the former Yugoslavia is still a test of the EU's ability to 'export' peace, democracy, social cohesion and economic growth in its immediate surroundings, i.e. to prove itself as an effective international player and 'nation-builder'. At the same time, it is a test of the ability of the US and EU to develop and implement joint concepts for the transformation of conflicts, thus also preserving the transatlantic partnership. The 'objects' of nation-building have, as always, little scope for asserting their ambitions. However, the rule of thumb still appears to apply that whoever maintains the best relations with the strongest external partner, the US, has the best prospects of realising at least part of its own goals.

The EU does, though, certainly have the power to take over the helm: it should summon up the courage to set a firm change of strategy in motion in relation to the West Balkans. Instead of the vague promise to examine, after a stabilisation and association process of indeterminate length, whether the countries of the region can be included in the group of EU candidates, an unambiguous assurance of admission should be given. The new strategy would gain credibility through financial resources being made available and EU structures adapted for the accelerated admission of the countries of the West Balkans. If there is clarity that the countries of the West Balkans are irreversibly on their way to joining the EU, it could then be much easier to stop any further territorial fragmentation and consolidate the existing political entities, thus enabling the outstanding 'national' problems to be resolved.

NOTES

1. This apposite description comes from the South-East Europe correspondent of *Süddeutsche Zeitung* (23 June 2003), Bernhard Küppers, in a commentary on the outcome of the EU Summit held in Thessaloniki on 19–21 June 2003, at which the 'Europeans' declined to grant the 'West Balkan States' the status of accession candidates.
2. Nationalists are, following the definition by Ernest Gellner (1983:1), those people that wish to bring about an identity between political and ethnic boundaries.
3. In his memoirs relating to the outbreak of the armed conflict, Hans-Dietrich Genscher (1995:966) attributes the responsibility for the decision to recognise Bosnia-Herzegovina under international law to the US: 'The

war in Bosnia-Herzegovina – the second Yugoslav war – began later, and the recognition of Bosnia-Herzegovina did not come about on our initiative – on the contrary. At the beginning of March 1992, Washington proposed that the USA and the European Community should act together.'

REFERENCES

Baker, James A., III (with Thomas M. DeFrank) (1995) *The Politics of Diplomacy, Revolution, War & Peace, 1989–1992* (New York).

Gellner, Ernest (1983) *Nations and Nationalism* (Ithaca, NY).

Genscher, Hans-Dietrich (1995) *Erinnerungen* (Berlin).

Gil-Robles, Alvaro (2002) *Kosovo: The Human Rights Situation and the Fate of Persons Displaced from their Homes* (Report by the Commissioner for Human Rights, Council of Europe, CommDH 11, October, Strasbourg).

Rice, Susan E. (2003) *The New National Security Strategy: Focus on Failed States* (The Brookings Institution Policy Brief No. 116, February, Washington, DC).

Schwarz, Axel (2002) 'Rückkehr des Absolutismus? – Machtstrukturen in UNMIK's Kosovo', *Südosteuropa*, Vol. 51, No. 10–12, pp. 527–42.

Triantaphyllou, Dimitrios (2003) *Balkans: The Transition from a reduced US Commitment* (Institute Note, Institute for Security Studies, March, Paris).

USIP (United States Institute of Peace) (2002) *Taking Stock and Looking Forward, Intervention in the Balkans and Beyond* (Special Report, February, Washington, DC).

9

Nigeria: The Oil State and the Crisis of Nation-building in Africa

Cyril I. Obi

At the height of the oil boom in the 1970s, a Nigerian military head of state allegedly boasted that money was no longer the country's problem, but how to spend it. This statement, whose veracity is shrouded in the realm of conjecture, nonetheless aptly captures the euphoria and sense of boundless wealth and power that petrodollars bestowed upon the Nigerian ruling class that had won a gruelling 30-month civil war in 1970. The Nigerian civil war, which was ostensibly fought to preserve the unity of the nation-state, was also partly provoked by the struggle between the political elite of the secessionist Biafra (Eastern region) and the rest of Nigeria (Northern, Western and Midwestern regions), over the control of the oil resources of the Niger Delta.

Before going further, it is important to explain that Nigeria is a multiethnic country. With an estimated population of 120 million people and over 250 ethnic groups of which three – the Hausa-Fulani, Yoruba and Igbo – are clearly demographically preponderant, politicised ethnicity has a profound impact on the oil state.

In spite of the victory of the forces of an integrative national(ist) ideology, divisive ethnicity reemerged in the context of economic and political crises following the collapse of global oil prices in the 1980s and 1990s and questioned the legitimacy of the oil-buoyed nation-state project. These protests were intensified by the harsh social consequences of the structural adjustment programme, military authoritarianism, and the passions unleashed by the annulment of the 12 June 1993 presidential elections. The elections were allegedly won by Moshood Abiola, a Yoruba man from the South-west, but were annulled by General Ibrahim Babangida, military head of state and a Nupe from the North. The crisis was further deepened with the ethnification of the postannulment protests, and the November 1993 coup, leading to the formation of various ethnic militia such as the O'Odua People's Congress (Yoruba), Arewa People's Congress (Hausa-

Fulani), and the Movement for the Actualisation of the Sovereign State of Biafra (Igbo). Ethnoregional sociopoliticocultural elite organisations such as the Afenifere (Yoruba), the Arewa Consultative Forum (Hausa-Fulani) and the Ohaneze Ndigbo (Igbo) among others, (re)emerged to mobilise their ethnic constituents to support their competing agenda for the Nigerian state. In spite of Nigeria's return to democracy in May 1999, pressures have continued to build up along ethnic, communal, regional and even religious lines thereby deepening the crisis of the nation-state.

The state became a site, as well as an actor in the struggles between factions of the various ethnic elites. In this regard, the three preponderant ethnic groups have largely controlled power at the centre since independence, while most of the minorities have either taken up the politics of protest, or aligned with one of the 'big three' to gain access to state patronage and resources. This is however not a new phenomenon given Nigeria's colonial history, and the divisions between the North and South which were administered by the British separately until the amalgamation of 1914. Equally relevant are the divisions between the North, the East and the West as factions of the emerging elite struggled for positions of advantage in a future independent Nigerian state by exploiting their ethnic and regional bases. At the heart of these divisions was the distrust and fear of domination of one by the other. These laid the foundations for the contradictions among the 'big three' in postcolonial Nigeria.

Since the mid 1990s, a faction of the Yoruba are demanding the decentralisation of federal power, alienated by the annulment of the 12 June 1993 presidential elections won by Abiola who was subsequently incarcerated and died in detention. This is impelled by their position that federal power has been allegedly monopolised by the Hausa-Fulani of the North to the disadvantage of the Yoruba. Factions from the ethnic minorities and the Igbo have also been demanding local autonomy and the convening of a sovereign national conference which is expected to provide them with a platform to negotiate for the devolution of power (and resources) to the various ethnic groups that are being emasculated by a highly centralised form of federalism.

It is, however, important to caution that reducing Nigerian politics to the level of ethnic determinism would be simplistic and wrong. For Nigerian politics is much more complex, with ethnic appearances masking deeper class, historical, personality, and economic interests. Ethnic politics is very fluid, with complex inter, intra and transclass alliances being forged and dissolved on the basis of political benefits and liabilities. In fundamental terms a lot depends on the exigencies of power and the determination to retain and gain control of state power.

Oil is the factor that cements Nigeria's ethnic pluralities and sociocultural diversities, just as struggles over oil threaten nation-building with the spectre of disintegration (Obi 2002:533–50). The post-civil war hegemonic national elite has stoutly resisted any attempt to restructure the Nigerian nation-state in order to protect its monopoly of oil power, best assured by the centralisation of state power and the politics of patronage. Thus, in spite of the protests of the excluded groups, their calls for decentralisation and a sovereign national conference in order to renegotiate the very basis of the Nigerian union, the hegemonic elite, fearful that giving in to such demands may lead to the unravelling of the Nigerian nation-state, but, more fundamentally, lead to the loss of their monopoly over oil power, continues to resist any real transfer of power and defends the integrative nationalist ideology.

This chapter critically examines the impact of Nigeria's total dependence on oil on the nation-building project. It explores the multiplicity of possibilities that revolve around the nexus between oil and the nation-state as a political and economic construct based on a European model, but largely controlled by an ethnically heterogeneous and oil-rentier political class. Perhaps the most critical of such possibilities relates to how relations of inclusion and exclusion from 'oil power' are constructed around a geography of power defined within the territorial space of the Nigerian state and reproduced by the global-national oil partnership. Thus, the oil sharpens the struggles between those who seek a radical redefinition of Nigeria in ways that respond to their demands for access to power and resource control, and a pan-Nigerian politicomilitary elite intending to defend its control of the petro-state at any cost.

The analysis that follows is arranged in four broad sections. A conceptual section explores the oil-state–nation nexus. It is followed by a historical background of Nigeria's emergence as a petro-state and its implications for the national question. The third section examines the internal and external dimensions of the Nigerian oil state and the crisis of nation-building, while the concluding section discusses the prospects for nation-building in the Nigerian and other African petro-states.

CONCEPTUAL ISSUES: OIL, THE STATE AND THE NATION

Oil, once described as 'the devil's excrement' (Karl 1999:32, quoting Juan Pablo Pérez, OPEC's founder), occupies a central position in the economics and politics of all oil-rich societies. This can be gleaned from the strong connection between the state as a specific modality of class domination and the economy in oil-rich contexts. It has been observed that oil tends to foster highly centralist and monopolistic political (and economic) forms (Morse 1999:14). As Dorraj argues (1995:125), drawing on cases of the petro-states of the Middle East and North Africa:

> While the influx of the petrodollar into the region since the 1960's has brought new wealth and progress, it has also emboldened the authoritarian regimes, supplying them with a new and sophisticated means of coercion and control, thus rendering them (in many cases), more autonomous from their societies.

It is apposite to place the petro-state in this context as one that is entirely dependent on rents or receipts from oil production and export. Due to the highly capital-intensive and enclave character of the oil industry in the developing world, and the domination of the production process and consumption by vertically integrated oil multinationals and the G8 countries, oil states are, in the main, reduced to being rent collectors and distributors. Therefore, in contexts like Nigeria, where Ake (1985:9) notes that 'the state is institutionally constituted in such a way that it enjoys little independence from the social classes, particularly the hegemonic classes', those who control the state also control oil. To a large extent, control of the Nigerian oil state bestows a lot of (unearned) wealth on the hegemonic classes, who then seek to retain power at any cost. Such power is often reinforced through patrimonial networks lubricated and reproduced through the distribution of oil largesse, while the 'opposition' is either bought off or repressed. The processes of inclusion and exclusion are primarily determined by access to state power, public office and the 'power of representation'.

From the foregoing it can be argued that in so far as substantive petro-dollars continue to flow into the coffers of the petro-state, that there is no incentive for the decentralisation of state power, accountability or any real development. Power remains concentrated in the hands of an oil bourgeoisie: national and global, more so as no real productive activity takes place outside of the enclave oil industry. Emphasis is on distributive or allocative activities, which are dictated more by control of the oil state rather than by merit, developmental or entrepreneurial productive activities. Oil is more of a booty or unearned income, further accentuated by the state's non-reliance on a local taxation base (Obi 2001:5).

The pervasive 'petrolisation' of politics and economics has implications for the nation. Apart from spawning centralised regimes that impose their sense of the nation on the state, it precludes the emergence of a genuine national capitalist class that will lead the process of an indigenous industrial revolution. By the same logic, it also precludes any real democratisation of society. The local dominant elite, while appropriating local symbols and discourses to legitimise its rule, remains dependent on external economic forces. To a large extent, power in oil states is highly personalised, thus fuelling a politics underscored by authoritarianism, distrust, instability and the use of coercive state power to keep any competition or the opposition in check. While this is obvious in the petro-states of North Africa, the Middle East and the Gulf, the situation in sub-Saharan Africa, particularly Nigeria, is a little more complex.

In Nigeria, although the post-civil war hegemonic class has imposed its sense of national unity on the country, the tensions between the heterogeneous and multiethnic nation and the state continue to pose challenges to the nation-state's legitimacy. The notion of a post-civil war homogeneous Nigerian nation (in the name of national unity) is being contested as a result of the intra-ruling class struggles for the control of oil and the alienation of the people by the Nigerian state. In this regard, the question of 'whose state' is coterminous with the questions of 'whose nation' and 'whose oil'. Thus, intraclass and ethnic divisions within the elite suggest that it has not been able to fully impose its hegemony on the Nigerian state. Therefore in the ensuing intraclass struggles, 'each faction gives itself a separate identity and mobilizes mass support using primordial loyalties such as ethnicity and religion' (Ake 1996:26–7).

Nationalist ideology is a legitimising tool in the hands of a hegemonic elite in petro-states. Due to the nexus between state and oil, any sudden interruption in oil flows or the fall in global oil prices is bound to send shock waves through the petrolised society. In such contexts, the refraction of global oil into the oil-rich social formation invariably leads to greater struggles over shrinking oil revenues, economic crises and the retreat of the welfare state, which undermine the legitimacy of the hegemonic nationalist ideology. The tensions between the state and the nation are exacerbated by either ethnicity or religion, or both, as groups jostle to gain to access to power and (oil) resources in a redefined national space and transformed social contract. Issues of equity, citizenship, public morality and culture define the struggles as new forces emerge to (re)claim the national space.

Oil is therefore central to understanding the crisis of nation-building in a multinational and multicultural context like Nigeria. The crisis of nation-building is characterised by the interrogation of the legitimacy and relevance of the nation-state by its constituent 'nations' and social groups. In this regard, the Nigerian state appears to be an imposition upon an ethnically heterogeneous society, trying hard to force through a project of national unity or homogenisation. In real terms, the project of homogenisation has not adopted representative or equitable methods; rather it has been imposed from above by relying on state power and centrally controlled institutions of national integration. Citizenship has thus been problematic as 'Nigerianhood' is mediated by ethnic origin, tagging 'excluded Nigerians' in contexts of competition, as strangers, settlers or non-indigenes. The agitation of the ethnic minorities of the oil-producing Niger Delta region for resource control and local autonomy, the communal conflicts over contested boundaries or shared natural resources including those involving indigenes versus settlers, the protests against marginalisation by almost every group, the demands for the adoption of Sharia law by predominantly Islamic states and the calls for a national conference to decentralise the Nigerian nation-state, all typify the tensions seething within Nigeria. In all this, elites of the diverse ethnic nations use identity as a bargaining chip or a weapon in the bid to renegotiate their position vis-à-vis access to power and oil and control of the nation-state. While the notion of an integrative nation-state project in Nigeria has been complicated by the class struggles around oil, the solution lies with a new and equitable national bargain involving all groups, based on the recognition of their local autonomy and the decentralisation of power.

THE NIGERIAN OIL STATE FROM A HISTORICAL PERSPECTIVE

The foundation of the Nigerian petro-state was laid by British colonial legislation of 1889, 1907 and 1914 that granted the monopoly of oil concessions in Nigeria to British and British-allied capital. It was under the 1914 Mineral Act that Shell was granted an oil exploration licence in 1938 covering the entire Nigerian mainland. Shell struck oil in 1956 and commenced oil exports in 1958 (Soremekun and Obi 1993). In 1959, more multinational oil corporations joined Shell in exploring for and producing oil in Nigeria, largely for the world market. Starting from 1958, when oil production was about 5,000 barrels a day, by 1974 it had risen to 2.26 million, with oil revenue far exceeding budgetary needs. At the peak of the oil boom in 1979, Nigeria produced 2.3 million barrels a day, before the oil shock (1981) forced cuts in production levels. Today, Nigeria produces about 2 million barrels of oil, but oil sales are at prices far below those of the oil-boom years. The expansion of Nigeria's oil production from the mid 1960s onwards was as a result of the high quality of Nigeria's crude oil and its proximity to the oil markets of Europe and North America.

Since the 1970s, oil has become the fiscal basis of the Nigerian state, providing over 95 per cent of its export earnings and 80 per cent of the revenues of the Nigerian state. The state became totally dependent on oil multinationals and the global oil market, with direct implications for Nigeria. Those who controlled the oil state concentrated power in themselves, and by doing so spawned zero-sum politics characterised by 'treachery, blackmail, violence and avarice' as they sought to reinforce their control of the state (Obi 2002a:535). The top echelon of the military also used their capture of the petro-state to become a part of the ruling class and thereby militarised politics. It is the push and pull – within factions of the national elite and between competing groups defined in terms of their ethnic or religious identity – over oil that lie at the heart of the threats to the Nigerian nation-state.

THE CRISIS OF THE NIGERIAN OIL STATE

The European model of the centralised nation-state forcefully imposed on Africa through colonial imperialism in the nineteenth and early twentieth centuries is in crisis. Ibrahim (2003:115) notes that in 'many parts of the world, the nation is finding it difficult and/or impossible to co-exist with the state. Nationalist, regional, ethnic and religious sentiments are rising, and the state is being challenged by these forces'. While Gana and Egwu (2003:xv) link the crisis of the nation-state project in Africa to the forces unleashed by globalisation, market reforms and democratisation, it would appear that the roots of the current crisis lie deeper in Africa's history, particularly in its colonial and decolonisation phases, which in turn account for the alienation of the postcolonial nation-state from the collective aspirations of its people. Describing the phenomenon as the curse of the nation-state, Davidson (2000:290) argues that:

> The state was not liberating and protective of its citizens, no matter what its propaganda claimed: on the contrary, its gross effect was constricting and exploitative, or else it simply failed to operate in any social sense at all.

At independence in 1960, the Nigerian nation-state had emerged in the legal sense, largely through the nationalist struggle and the indigenisation of a British-modelled colonial state. The Nigerian state was an imposition and not the outcome of a voluntary union of the multiethnic nations in Nigeria. The British did not integrate the various precolonial social formations they forced into the colonial state of Nigeria, rather they created division and distrust among Nigerians through indirect rule and different administrative policies towards Northern and Southern Nigeria.

The elite that led the decolonisation process in the relatively short time of nine years, 1951 to 1960, won an independent Nigerian nation-state in which Nigerians did not have a well-developed vision of nationhood, even as the adopted federal system hinged upon strong ethnoregional units and a weak centre. Thus, the Nigerian nation-state at independence was more apparent than real, with the state only beginning to impose its will on the nation(s). As Gana argues (2003:18–19), 'national integration was never on the agenda of the Nigerian successors to the state apparatus'. In his view, the 'national question was not posed until the Biafran crisis', thus lending credence to the earlier view that the shift from agrarian cash crop to oil-based accumulation also had a profound impact on nation-building in Nigeria. It was with the advent of oil as a vital contributor to the country's revenues that the regionalised political elite began to take on board 'a totalizing state-centred project based on the integrative needs of the nation state' (Mustapha 1998:27). Two factors were behind this: firstly, the coups of January and July 1966, which brought the military to power and led to the transfer of its centralising and commandist ethos to the Nigerian polity. Secondly, the decline of the agrarian economy which was strong in the erstwhile three regions that also coincided with the 'big three' (Northern-Hausa-Fulani, Eastern-Igbo and Western-Yoruba). The rise of the oil economy that was largely concentrated in the ethnic minority areas of the Niger Delta meant that in the absence of an economic base for the ethnopolitical elite in the three regions, Niger Delta oil became a unifying locus for Pax Nigeriana. It also meant that the post-civil war hegemonic elite had to take control of the oil in the ethnic minority areas outside of their own regions in order to reproduce themselves as a national ruling class. This explains how oil became the fuel of a centralised unifying nation-state project, which received a boost with the victory of federalist forces at the end of the civil war. By this victory, Nigeria's military rulers succeeded in their bid to control the petro-state. This was legitimised through an ideology of national development – building a strong and united Nigeria, clearly reminiscent of the slogan of the civil war: 'To Keep Nigeria One is a Task that Must be Done'.

The impact of oil on nation-building in Nigeria after the war was that the (centralised) state became the ultimate prize in politics. Using the slogan of national development the Nigerian state became central to oil-based accumulation and allocation. Partly to weaken the regions as loci of power (and possible opposition to federal might), the military abolished the four regions and replaced them incrementally with 12, 19, 21 and eventually 36 states (regions) that were virtually dependent on the centre for oil largesse. While this was partly designed to move the locus of struggle between factions of the elite from the centre to other tiers of the federation, it was also meant to reinforce the formidable power wielded by the oil state over the heterogeneous nation, so that the former would homogenise the latter through integrative nation-building.

The fall in oil receipts from an average of 10 billion dollars annually in the 1970s to about 5 billion in the 1980s and 1990s had a devastating impact on Nigeria. It led to intensified pressures for the redistribution of shrinking oil revenues by those who were marginalised from power. Ethnic and religious identities were reinforced and used to challenge the legitimacy of a homogenising nation-state project. Olukoshi and Agbu (1996:75) note that in the 1990s, Nigeria's unity could no longer be taken for granted, as groups demanded the restructuring of the Nigerian federation to promote 'greater autonomy and provide for a politically and financially weaker centre'. Of note were the calls by the ethnic minorities and social movements of the Niger Delta for autonomy and redistribution of oil in their favour as those who contributed the most – through oil to the Nigerian purse. They interrogated the logic of 'national unity' which denied them access to and control of the oil produced from their region, and waged a local and global struggle against the Nigerian state. This directly threatened the legitimacy of the state and its role in oil accumulation and distribution, leading to the repression of protest movements in the Niger Delta.

The external dimension of the crisis of nation-building is linked to the dependence of the Nigerian petro-state on foreign oil multinationals and the global oil market. The limited autonomy of the Nigerian state in relation to external extractive (and pollutive) forces also implies that the state is not free from the struggle between these forces of economic globalisation and those of local resistance in the Niger Delta. In this regard, the petro-state alienates some of its own citizens (nationals) and sides with oil multinationals in exploiting and repressing them. This often portrays the state to the oil minorities as not being representative of their interests, wherefore its predatory instincts should be curtailed by the decentralisation of the hegemonic nation-state project.

PROSPECTS FOR NIGERIA AND OTHER PETRO-STATES IN AFRICA

The steady fall in oil prices has fuelled crises in African petro-states with varying degrees of intensity. In Nigeria, in spite of the existence of several homogenising federal institutions and policies, the unity of the country remains a contested terrain. The reconstruction of ethnic and regional identities, numerous clan and communal conflicts, some of which pitch indigenes versus settlers (Mustapha 1998:47) continue to undermine the process of national integration. This crisis can also be explained in part by the politics of a rich 'politicomilitary elite' that has captured the Nigerian state and widened the gap between it and the nation. This elite – a coalition of civilian politicians and (ex-)military officers – has not been able to homogenise its own nationalism beyond imposing a centralised logic of accumulation and the appropriation of oil rents, while it manipulates ethnicity and religion in its factional politics, thus contributing to conflict and crises.

Across Africa, petro-states appear to be immersed in the cycle of 'permanent transitions' (White and Taylor 2001:323), marked by non-transitions, truncated transitions, manipulated transitions and the lack of democracy. In the well-known case of Algeria, the military annulled elections in 1992, when it appeared that an Islamist party that would desecularise the Algerian state and gain control of oil power was heading for electoral victory. A year later, the Nigerian military annulled the 1993 presidential elections, when the politicomilitary elite had reservations about the alleged winner. In Libya and Gabon, no political transitions have taken place for a long time, while Angola is only just recovering from three decades of civil war.

The prospects for the petro-state in promoting a crisis-free nation-building project appear to be problematic. The international community will likely continue to tolerate permanent transitions and the volatile fallouts of the crises of the African petro-states and their lack of real democracy and development, in so far as oil keeps flowing into the global markets, thus pushing further away the possibilities for the resolution of the national question.

REFERENCES

Ake, Claude (1985) 'The Nigerian State: Antimonies of a Periphery Formation', in Claude Ake (ed.), *Political Economy of Nigeria* (London/Lagos).

Ake, Claude (1996) 'The Political Question', in Oyeleye Oyediran (ed.), *Governance and Development in Nigeria. Essays in Honour of Billy J. Dudley* (Ibadan).

Davidson, Basil (2000) *The Black Man's Burden: Africa and the Curse of the Nation-State* (Ibadan).

Dorraj, Manochehr (1995) 'State, Petroleum and Democratisation in the Middle East and North Africa', in Manochehr Dorraj (ed.), *The Changing Political Economy of the Third World* (Boulder, CO).

Gana, Aaron (2003): 'Federalism and the National Question in Nigeria: A Theoretical Exploration', in Aaron Gana and Samuel Egwu (eds), *Federalism in Africa, Volume One: Framing the National Question* (Lawrenceville, NJ/Asmara).

Gana, Aaron and Samuel Egwu (2003) 'The Crisis of the Nation-State in Africa and the Challenge of Federalism', in Aaron Gana and Samuel Egwu (eds), *Federalism in Africa, Volume One: Framing the National Question* (Lawrenceville, NJ/Asmara).

Ibrahim, Jibrin (2003) 'Ethno-Religious Limits to the Construction of Federalism in Africa: Yugoslavia and Nigeria Compared', in Aaron Gana and Samuel Egwu (eds), *Federalism in Africa, Volume One: Framing the National Question* (Lawrenceville, NJ/Asmara).

Karl, Terry (1999) 'The Perils of the Petro-state: Reflections on the Paradox of Plenty', *Journal of International Affairs*, Vol. 53, No. 1 (Fall), p. 32.

Morse, Edward (1999) 'A New Political Economy of Oil?', *Journal of International Affairs*, Vol. 53, No. 1 (Fall), pp. 1–48.

Mustapha, Abdul (1998) 'Identity Boundaries, Ethnicity and National Integration in Nigeria', in Okwudiba Nnoli (ed.), *Ethnic Conflicts in Africa* (Dakar).

Obi, Cyril (2001) *The Changing Forms of Identity Politics in Nigeria under Economic Adjustment: The Case of the Oil Minorities of the Niger Delta* (Nordiska Afrikainstitutet, Research Report No. 119).

Obi, Cyril (2002) 'Ethnic Minority Agitation and the Specter of National Disintegration', in Toyin Falola (ed.), *Nigeria in the Twentieth Century* (Durham, NC).

Olukoshi, Adebayo and Osita Agbu (1996) 'The Deepening Crisis of Nigerian Federalism and the Future of the Nation-State', in Adebayo Olukoshi and Liisa Laakso (eds), *Challenges to the Nation-State in Africa* (Nordiska Afrikainstitutet in cooperation with Institute of Development Studies, University of Helsinki, Uppsala).

Soremekun, Kayode and Cyril Obi (1993) 'The Changing Pattern of Private Foreign Investments in the Nigerian Oil Industry', *African Development*, Vol. XVIII, No. 3.

White, Gregory and Scott Taylor (2001) 'Well-Oiled Regimes: Oil and Uncertain Transitions in Algeria and Nigeria', *Review of African Political Economy*, No. 89. pp. 323–44.

Part III

The Politics of Nation-building

10
Between Projectitis and the Formation of Countervailing Power – NGOs in Nation-building Processes

Jeanette Schade

Non-governmental organisations (NGOs)[1] play a central role in many of the nation-building concepts initiated by the international community and its players. The United Nations, its special organisations as well as state and regional institutions for emergency aid and development cooperation work together with NGOs to implement their humanitarian assistance and long-term development programmes and consult with each other. Meant by nation-building in this context are, primarily, the maintaining of peace and reconstruction.

The aim is for NGOs to contribute towards nation-building by promoting social and political integration. They can, for example, help with the reintegration of civil war refugees by being involved in repatriation programmes or with the stabilisation of the social situation by providing basic services for the population in (post-)conflict situations; establishing infrastructures quickly and flexibly for reconstruction work; setting up schools and training centres to avoid losing valuable human resources; influencing the form of a new political order by lending their support for the processing of war crimes, legal and political consideration of marginalised groups, equal rights and equal treatment of women, land rights or transparent and democratic state structures, thus helping to overcome social rifts.

The reason for donors increasingly enlisting the assistance of NGOs for parts of the nation-building process lies mainly in the fact that NGOs offer an alternative to the often dysfunctional state structures in failed states or post-conflict countries. However, it also reflects the general trend since the end of the East–West conflict towards granting development cooperation resources increasingly to NGOs rather than to the governments of the target countries – whether to avoid corruption and mismanagement, to promote pluralism and human rights or to exert specific influence on political development. This change of paradigm makes NGOs a central component of the international aid and development industry, granting them previously unknown access to material and political resources.

Nation-building does, however, have another, historically older dimension that stands in the way of international reconstruction endeavours: wars are likewise part of the nation-building process and NGOs and, in particular, the instrumentalisation of their resources can also play a role in these.

NATION-BUILDING AND NGOs IN (POST-)CONFLICT SITUATIONS

NGOs in (post-)conflict situations are viewed almost exclusively in the literature from the point of view of emergency refugee aid and their role in the prevention of humanitarian disasters. Literature has now also been published in relation to negative effects of the aid and development industry for social stability and peace processes. The criticism focuses on the instrumentalisation of aid for political and military purposes, its interaction with the war economy, the prolonging of conflicts as well as the exacerbation and cementing of emergency humanitarian situations (e.g. Anderson 1999). This literature clearly shows that, despite the humanitarian imperative to treat those in need equally, regardless of their ethnic, religious, political or other affiliations, humanitarian aid is all too quickly instrumentalised by conflicting parties in times of war and that the principle of neutrality is losing touch with reality.[2]

NGOs bring much-sought-after and extensive resources into crisis regions in the form of aid goods. The distribution of these goods can benefit warring parties, influence the course of war and strengthen or weaken the position of social players and groups in postwar times. Humanitarian aid therefore frequently contains – intentionally or unintentionally – a political or military dimension. This is demonstrated, in relation to the war in Iraq, by the vehemence with which NGOs refused to be 'embedded' by the allied forces in the same way as journalists and be used for image-enhancement purposes (Byman 2001; Bierdel and Kap Anamur 2003).

However, the literature hardly deals explicitly with how the positive and negative aspects of humanitarian aid in war situations relate to nation-building. Nonetheless, there are a number of aspects that can also play a role for nation-building:

- Food aid distributed by NGOs can be used to win over the loyalty of the population; to make opposing sections of the population dependent and, therefore, submissive; to manipulate migratory movements and selectively steer people into desired regions (Prendergast 1996:19–20). Such settlement-policy measures can serve to weaken or strengthen the predominant position of political opponents with competing nation-building concepts or secessionist ambitions.

- Food aid, just like other aid goods, is diverted to provide for one's own military. NGOs report from their operations in Sudan, Liberia, Tajikistan, Bosnia, Somalia, Rwanda, Angola and other conflict regions of aid goods being purloined or extorted as road tolls, to provide for soldiers or to be sold in order to procure weapons (Anderson 1999:38). In Somalia and Sudan, NGOs estimate that up to 80 per cent of aid was lost through theft and misappropriation (Byman 2001:99). International aid payments can also be legally taken into account to reserve more funds from the state budget for military expenditure (Barnes 2000).

- Refugee camps, also often run by NGOs, can be used as a cover for military mobilisation and thus gain strategic advantage. The security requirements for protecting refugee camps and aid goods against theft and robbery can make NGOs victims of extortion for protection money, thus enriching and strengthening parties in the conflict.

- With their information-gathering work for the media and decision-makers, NGOs influence the perception of conflicts and the reactions of the public and governments abroad, which can, for their part, exert influence on the course of war and negotiations (e.g. by sending or withdrawing forces or aid payments) (Clapham 2000:230).

These and other measures are suitable, within the context of nation-building, for promoting integration or disintegration, consolidating one's own military strength or destabilising one's opponents. The extent of the impact of this strategic aid dimension in individual cases depends on other external and internal factors, such as the political leaning of the donors, interaction with other types of aid (e.g. military aid) and the internal political balance of power.

NGOs, RECONSTRUCTION AND NATION-BUILDING

The reconstruction phase is linked, in particular, with the practical, organisational aspects of nation-building. Nationwide physical infrastructure and communication networks are needed to boost the national economy, as well as interaction and integration of social groups. Certain basic supplies and services are necessary to ensure social stability and facilitate productive employment. What is required above all is state-building, that is the establishment of an administrative apparatus to successfully manage functions and investments in the areas of security, the economy, transport, health, education, etc.

The state capacities in many post-conflict countries are, however, still too weak to perform these functions. International aid attempts to compensate for this deficiency at several levels – aid for the military, the police, infrastructure, humanitarian issues, etc. NGOs provide basic supplies and services as a matter of priority for as long as state structures or market mechanisms are not yet in a position to do so, though this provisional arrangement does frequently become a permanent substitute for state or public action (e.g. in Afghanistan and Palestine). This trend is encouraged by the change in paradigm concerning the policy pursued by donors in awarding funds, with NGOs frequently preferred over governments in the target countries. What initially has (or could have) the effect of easing the burden on weak state structures leads, in many case, to NGOs and local governments competing with each other, which can impact negatively on state-building. However, NGOs do not only have a double-edged effect on the latter in frequent cases, they also impact on the development of local markets.

NGOs AS PART OF THE MARKETS

The resources available to the NGO sector not only make it a potentially efficient service provider, it also becomes an attractive economic factor and labour market segment. NGOs need local skilled personnel, translators, packers, drivers, cleaning staff, etc. In the economically desolate region of Palestine, the NGO sector provided around 25,000 jobs in 2001 (MIFTAH 2001). In Afghanistan, the Swedish Committee for Afghanistan ran 168 clinics in 18 provinces in 2002, had around 6,000 Afghan personnel and was one of the largest private employers in the country (Schenkenberg van Mierop 2002:3).

NGOs also create indirect employment through their demand for property, office equipment and accommodation for their external personnel, as well as maintenance requirements for vehicles, etc. The prerequisite is that the goods required are (can be) purchased from local producers rather than being imported. Economic stimulus of this type is initially something positive.

The substantial demand created by NGOs can, however, distort prices or even drive them excessively high. This concerns, in particular, real estate, rents and qualified labour. What can be particularly negative for nation-building are the high salaries that international NGOs and UN organisations (can) pay in comparison to the local country. This leads to a brain drain from the state sector to the non-profit and development sector, which robs the state apparatus (and frequently local NGOs) of capacities. Ignatieff (2003:100) speaks of 'capacity-confiscation'. Highly qualified local personnel often work merely as drivers or translators for Western development agencies, with the result that qualifications valuable for nation-building are left untapped (Guest 2000).

Given that the economy is a particularly important area of social interaction, NGOs can, as employers and major customers, also contribute to the integration, or even disintegration, of social structures. If lucrative jobs and contracts are awarded along established conflict lines, this can help exacerbate social tensions and discrepancies. In Mozambique, for example, most of the qualified personnel were also supporters of the governing party, Frelimo, while the workers from the areas controlled by the resistance movement, Renamo, were more poorly trained. Only NGOs that also took on Renamo personnel, thus introducing social tensions into the organisation by way of mixed teams, contributed – where successful – towards integration and reducing or avoiding social tensions between the former adversaries (Halvorsen 1995).

One extremely ambivalent item of the aid and development economy for a nation-building process is security. NGOs need security for their aid goods, facilities and personnel. If this cannot be adequately ensured because of a lack of state monopoly of force or international peace-keeping troops, NGOs frequently have to depend on private security services or pay protection money to locally dominant warlords in order to simply not be attacked by them. Since this strengthens the warlords both economically and politically and makes it more difficult to assert a state monopoly of force, it helps to preserve the structures of the war economy that still exist.

NGOs, GOVERNMENTS AND STATE-BUILDING

Ideally, NGOs become involved where the state's social service provision structures are not yet functioning. Newly emerging (and also established) governments and state machineries can, however, find themselves competing with individual NGOs or the NGO sector as a whole at several levels: they compete for international aid funds, for the personnel and technical resources for their organisation, in the structuring of the system for providing social services, and therefore also for the recognition and loyalty of the population. The relationship between governments and NGOs is thus often strained in view of the transfer of competencies and resources brought about by the donors. This is particularly evident in Afghanistan.

> [In Afghanistan] within the government (ministries and ACA [Afghan Assistance Coordination Authority]), the question has emerged as to how to 'control' the NGOs. There are repeated rumours of hostility, or at least resentment, from government representatives towards NGOs. These feelings may have been fed by the fact that for more than a decade, NGOs have been able to operate in Afghanistan in a vacuum, bypassing the central government, and sometimes even working against them. Presently, NGOs outstrip the operational capacity of any government body by far and this will probably remain so at least for the next two years. It should come as no surprise that this situation may further trigger hostility and tensions. (Schenkenberg van Mierop 2002:12)

The preference shown by the international donors for NGOs does, in fact, signify the taking of a decision of general principle concerning the system for the supply of social services. This no longer comes under the area of responsibility of the government; rather it is being privatised via NGOs. In Palestine, for example, local NGOs with foreign support provided 60 per cent of basic medical care services and ran 42 per cent of the hospitals, 90 per cent of the centres for the disabled and 95 per cent of the preschool education facilities before the outbreak of the second intifada (MIFTAH 2001). Some 70 per cent of the healthcare services in Afghanistan are provided by NGOs (Ridde 2002:22). However, services in the health, social and education domains are important sources of social recognition for the state apparatus, especially in poor countries. Legitimation resources and social policy control instruments are therefore being taken away from the state by NGOs. For ideological reasons, NGOs do not always share the political preferences of the donors, although they benefit from them. Such NGOs characterised by social welfare state ideas do, however, frequently get caught up in conflicts of objectives in rigidly governed developing countries. In Palestine, for instance, a large number of NGOs favour a Palestinian state that performs important social and development policy functions nationwide while at the same time being sceptical towards the policy pursued by the autonomous authority:

> ... in the absence of democratic rules of the game, NGOs may view it is being in their own interest to retain their own separate institutional sphere and maintain a strong role in service provision, even at the expense of their own ideological views. (Hanafi and Tabar forthcoming)

The present policy for awarding funds is resulting, in the final analysis, in a conflict surrounding the distribution of resources and control of their use. According to the Afghan transitional government, for example, only US$296 million (16 per cent) of the US$1.84 billion awarded between January 2002 and March 2003 went directly to the government. Most of the money was distributed to the UN (US$562 million) and international NGOs (US$446 million) (Transitional Government of Afghanistan 2003:3). Cooperation and coordination between the government and NGOs would be an appropriate way to strengthen state sovereignty in the area of social policy despite the lack of capacities and turn NGO work rather into relief of the strain than into competition. Although mechanisms for this already existed in part, according to Nazir Shahidi (2002), Deputy Minister of Reconstruction in Afghanistan, the NGOs did not make allowances for the government priorities elaborated in the National Development Framework. They were seen to be unwilling to cooperate and coordinate. Conversely, NGOs complain of a lack of readiness to cooperate and an inability to coordinate on the part of the government (Schenkenberg van Mierop 2002:11–12) and see themselves as being occasionally excluded by the international community through the introduction of new funding mechanisms (Afghanistan Reconstruction Trust Fund) (Ridde 2002:22), or they question the national ownership of the National Development Framework (ActionAid 2003).

Although the awarding of resources via NGOs safeguards their use for social rather than, for example, military purposes to a great extent, it is not a guarantee against corruption and mismanagement or for the most effective allocation. According to Mark Sedra (2003:4), the preference for NGOs has led in Afghanistan to a '"projectization" of the reconstruction process, a fragmentation of the process along institutional and project lines'. The Afghan government is also said to prefer infrastructure projects that create employment to social measures, as the former would, at the same time, provide alternative income to those engaged in armed service for the warlords (Ignatieff 2003:11). This could help to break the cycle of the war economy and weaken the warlords' local monopoly of force.

Where NGO projects enable warlords to make a mark politically, this also weakens young governments and weak state machineries. The northern Afghan warlord, Rashid Dostum, for instance, enjoys carrying out the official opening of schools and other facilities in the region he controls and has made political capital out of the return of hundreds of prisoners of war who, without the care of the Red Cross, would otherwise have died beforehand in his prisons (Ignatieff 2003:81–2). In contrast to the government in Kabul, warlords repeatedly manage, by virtue of their regional monopoly of force, to take the political credit for NGO projects. In this way, NGOs help the warlords – intentionally or unintentionally – to obtain social legitimacy, support their promoted regional and/or ethnic self-conception instead of a national one and thus confirm the image of the interim President Karzai as merely 'the mayor of Kabul'.

NGOs AND NATIONAL POLICY OBJECTIVES

There are also counterexamples to the relationship potentially leading to conflict and competition between NGOs and the government in failed states, as outlined above. In Myanmar (Burma), the government makes use of the NGO sector to consolidate its nation-building project. In 1993, the military dictatorship's State Peace and Development Council (SPDC; previously the State Law and Order Restoration Council/SLORC) established the Union Solidarity and Development Association (USDA), a (quasi-)NGO loyal to the government, with the mandate to realise 'our three main national causes – non-disintegration of the Union, non-disintegration of national solidarity, and perpetuation of sovereignty' and an ideology legitimising the dominant role of the national armed forces in this nation-building process (Coakley 1998:2).

USDA is extremely active at local level in the areas of community development and adult education. It draws large numbers of members (estimated at 5 million in 1996) and offers a range of advantages, e.g. regarding access to jobs and university places. At the same time, the government uses the organisation to mobilise people against political opponents, who could allegedly present a danger to the unity and stability of the country (though in fact to the regime's power). In 1999, according to Purcell, many donors and external NGOs looking for local NGO partners were still cooperating with the USDA and its extensive network, thus helping to strengthen its structures – at the expense of small local NGOs and the Christian Church and Buddhist networks (Purcell 1999:86, 97). USDA is therefore not only an effective instrument for integration and control of the population, safeguarding power and asserting a nation-building concept from above; it also proves a useful body for channelling the resources and activities of foreign NGOs and donor organisations.

USDA is an effective element of the nation-building strategy in Myanmar principally because, in contrast to most NGOs, it is nationally oriented in terms of objective and ideology. This is not necessarily a characteristic of quasi-state organisations, nor is it exclusive to them. The Afghan peace initiative, Afghanistan Peace Association (APA), expressly supports national unity and overcoming conflicts between the different groups of the multiethnic state: 'Internal fighting and shooting at compatriots, in the view of the APA, is considered anti-Afghan, anti-national and anti-unity' (see <www.afghanistanpeace.com>). A private initiative will, however, only rarely be able to compete with a state-sponsored organisation in the establishment of national structures.

ARE NGOs ESSENTIAL FOR NATION-BUILDING?

The role of NGOs in nation-building is a contradictory one and therefore difficult to assess. In times of war, it depends on the skill of the parties involved in the conflict as to how they make use of NGOs for their strategies. NGOs rarely play an active role in this phase – if they want to adhere to the principle of neutrality. If NGOs actually do (or want to) become actively and effectively involved in the nation-building process during a war, those with the greatest resources and influence, at least, would have to decide to support one of the parties in the conflict. It is precisely this, however, which is inconsistent with the principle of neutrality, the humanitarian imperative and the endeavour of many NGOs not to be instrumentalised – though the latter can often not be avoided in armed conflicts, especially where there is a causal link between need and force. NGOs do, however, have the possibility to avoid being consumed by the conflicting parties through not offering any more aid, a measure that some NGOs also actually threaten and practice.

In the reconstruction phase, there are likewise two sides to the role of the NGOs. In the case of state machineries that are still unable to act or are weak, they are indispensable for the rapid provision of social services while, on the other hand, they can be an obstacle to the development of functional state structures because of the brain, loyalty and capacity drain. After all, they do not guarantee any systematic, comprehensive provision of services to the population as a whole. For these reasons, there are increasing demands for international resources to be allocated directly to governments again or to at least restrain the role and autonomy of NGOs.

> Although their [NGOs'] role will remain important – particularly with respect to the continuing need for humanitarian aid – they will also need to accept that being 'sidelined' is a positive development if this means that the reconstruction agenda is being led by a legitimate Afghan government. ... Will they be prepared to relinquish some of their sovereignty and profile? (Goodhand and Ludin 2002:32)

The direct responsibility of NGOs for the course of nation-building should not be overrated. Other external factors and players perform more important roles. It is the donors and not they themselves who decide on the amount of resources that are made available to them and which can cause them to potentially compete with the government. Nor do their possible negative effects for state-building, for example the brain drain, apply specifically to NGOs; this is also true for development cooperation institutions as a whole. UN organisations and foreign embassies pay even better salaries than NGOs. Military aid, arms trading and foreign interests also carry more weight where the arming of parties involved in the conflict is concerned. The failure to establish the state's monopoly of force in Afghanistan is not the fault of the NGOs.

The cooperation difficulties between governments and NGOs cannot be blamed exclusively on the NGOs; these can also be attributed to sensitivities of the ruling elite that go beyond meaningful considerations concerning the nation-building process. Nonetheless, it should be acknowledged that the image many NGOs have of themselves, characterised by remoteness from the state, and their exaggerated concern about abuse by the state can hinder the development of constructive cooperation.

However, there are also structural reasons for the work of NGOs in the area of nation-building being of only moderate relevance. Disregarding quasi-state institutions like the USDA for a moment, only very few NGOs have national structures and strategies and only rarely do they take account of or propagate, like APA for instance, ideas that have explicitly national terms of reference. On the contrary, their central ideas are universal, reaching beyond the national level to the humanitarian imperative or the concept of human rights. This doesn't necessarily harm nation-building. But does it help it?

NOTES

1. Meant by non-governmental organisations (NGOs) here are private, national as well as international non-profit organisations involved in the areas of humanitarian aid and development cooperation.
2. With regard to the humanitarian imperative, cf. the *Code of Conduct for the International Red Cross and Red Crescent Movement* (ICRC et al. 1994). The biggest but not all NGOs involved in emergency aid are bound by this voluntary code.

REFERENCES

ActionAid (2003) *The National Development Framework* (Research Project) <www.actionaid.org/resources/emergencies/emergencies.shtml>.

Anderson, Mary (1999) *Do No Harm. How Aid Can Support Peace – or War* (London).

Barnes, Sam (2000) 'Feeding the War Machine in Ethiopia', *Boston Sunday Globe*, 28 May <www.escribe.com/culture/dehai-news/m9486.html>.

Bierdel, Elias and Kap Anamur (2003) *Wie erleben die Menschen im Irak den Krieg?* (Interview on WDR 5 morgenecho, 28.03.2003).

Byman, Daniel (2001) 'Uncertain Partners: NGOs and the Military', *Survival*, Vol. 43, No. 2 (Summer), pp. 27–114.

Clapham, Christopher (2000) *Africa and the International System. The Politics of State Survival*, 5th edn (Cambridge).

Coakley, V. (1998) 'Politics of Stability: Co-opting Burma's Civil Society through the USDA', *Burma Issues*, Vol. 8, No. 10 (October), pp. 2–4.

Goodhand, Jonathan and Jawed Ludin (2002) 'The Afghanistan Reconstruction Trust Fund: a "Lack-of-Trust" Fund for Afghanistan?', in *Humanitarian Exchange*, publ. by Overseas Development Institute, London (November), pp. 31–2.

Guest, Iain (2000): *Misplaced Charity Undermines Kosovo's Self-Reliance* (Overseas Development Council) <www. globalsolidarity.org/articles/mischar. html>.

Halvorsen, Kate (1995) *Reintegration Efforts in a Post-War Context: The Activities of the Danish Refugee Council and Norwegian Refugee Council in Mozambique* <www.cdainc.com/dnh/publications/casestudies/lcppCase11Mozambique. pdf>.

Hanafi, Sari and Linda Tabar (forthcoming) *Donors, International Organizations, Local NGOs. The Emergence of the Palestinian Globalized Elite* (Ramallah [Arabic]/London [English]).

ICRC (International Committee of the Red Cross) et al. (1994) *Code of Conduct for the International Red Cross and Red Crescent Movement and NGOs in Disaster Relief* (Geneva).

Ignatieff, Michael (2003) *Empire Lite. Nation-Building in Bosnia, Kosovo and Afghanistan* (London).

MIFTAH (Palestinian Initiative for the Promotion of Global Dialogue and Democracy) (2001) *The Changing Role of NGOs in Palestine* <www.miftah. org/Display.cfm?DocId=84&CategoryId=4>.

Prendergast, John (1996) *Frontline Diplomacy. Humanitarian Aid and Conflict in Africa* (London).

Purcell, Marc (1999) '"Axe-handles or Willing Minions?": International NGOs in Burma', Burma Centre Netherlands (BCN)/ Transnational Institute (TNI) (ed.), *Strengthening Civil Society in Burma* (Chiang Mai/Thailand).

Ridde, Valéry (2002) 'Why a Trust Fund Won't Work in Afghanistan', *Humanitarian Exchange*, publ. by Overseas Development Institute (London) July, pp. 22–3.

Schenkenberg van Mierop, Ed (2002) *NGO Coordination and Some Other Relevant Issues in the Context of Afghanistan from an NGO Perspective* <www.db. idpproject.org/Sites/idpSurvey.nsf/wViewCountries/2E3B5DE B1BE7387FC1256B9E00338A1F/$file/NGO_Coordination_9April02.pdf>.

Sedra, Mark (2003) 'The "Day After" in Iraq. Lessons from Afghanistan', *Foreign Policy in Focus* (March) <www.fpif.org/papers/iraqrebuild2003.html>.

Shahidi, Nazir (2002) *Erfolg oder Enttäuschung? Probleme beim Wiederaufbau in Afghanistan* (Interview on WDR 5 morgenecho, 26.11.2002).

Transitional Government of Afghanistan (2003) *Analysis of Aid Flows to Afghanistan* (as per: 2 April 2003) <www.af/resources/mof/adf-ahsf-artf/ Aid_Analysis-with_graphs.pdf>.

11
External Nation-building vs Endogenous Nation-forming – A Development Policy Perspective

Ulrike Hopp and Adolf Kloke-Lesch

The development policy debate over the past few years has no doubt been influenced primarily by the phenomena of globalisation, breakdown of the state and internal national conflicts. Although these processes are part of the challenges that many developing countries have to face, they also represent conditions under which development policy has to work. The background and consequences of September 11, 2001 plus the conflict in Iraq have underscored the complexity of these phenomena.

With the ever-growing cross-border interlinking of trade and financial flows in particular, as well as increased pressure concerning liberalisation and privatisation, plus the constantly and ever more visibly widening gulf in economic and social conditions both between and within regions and countries, the call for effective statism and social equalisation is becoming louder. Protecting one's citizens internally and representing their interests externally requires a functioning state. At the same time, states do not only enjoy rights in a multilateral system, they also have responsibilities and obligations, for example in relation to internal state implementation of internationally agreed norms and standards (Maull 2002).

In a large number of developing countries, however, the relevance of efficient, democratic statism is set against state dysfunctionality, increasing state failure or even the breakdown of the state. Depending on the method used to count them, there are anything up to 40 weak states, with a good dozen countries heading toward state failure or already deemed to have failed. Seen against this background, the principle developed in the 1990s according to which development cooperation was to take place with *good-performing countries* is being increasingly watered down. Concepts for development cooperation with *poor-performing countries* have been drawn up by the World Bank, the Organisation for Economic Co-operation and Development

(OECD) and bilateral donors in order to find ways out of the spiral of failure. Ultimately, international peace-keeping missions have been required precisely in those places where states have no longer fulfilled their responsibility with regard to human rights and the security of their citizens.

On top of this, we have become increasingly aware of violent conflicts and wars both within states and in the context of regional conflict systems since the end of the Cold War. These frequently have supraregional or even global repercussions, obstructing and even preventing sustainable development.

Besides the numerous development policy contributions towards dealing with conflicts in a civil manner, the concept of nation-building is also addressed in the search for answers to these challenges, with this specifically mentioned as one of the tasks in so-called *complex emergencies*, for example in Cambodia, the Balkans or the present East Timor. In the case of Afghanistan, it is seen at the same time as an effective means of combating terrorism (Rotberg 2002:139–40). However, contributions towards nation-building are also the subject of discussion in less dramatic surroundings. It is possible that the term is enjoying growing popularity because it promises a less technocratic objective, in contrast to approaches like that of the OECD on 'structural stability'. Furthermore, nation-building evidently serves to kill two birds with one stone by combining state-forming as an answer to dysfunctional statism with a cohesion strategy designed to help counter external and alienating influences as well as division and fragmentation within society.

However, there is a wide divergence in the understanding of the process of nation-building and of the possibilities regarding external support. This discourse is burdened by a widespread – and not unfounded – ambivalent attitude towards the term, which is often associated with the reconstruction after World War II, the decolonialisation phase, the demise of the Soviet Union and Yugoslavia or an especially pronounced leaning towards external interests. Corresponding restraint can be found not only in the European discussion; it is also evident in the debate in the US, which otherwise proceeds in a rather more pragmatic manner when gearing the objectives of its external support towards the National Security Strategy, for example (Rice 2002).

A range of views are emerging in the debate, which can essentially be divided between two poles:

- On the one side, nation-building is seen in the context of or even equated with state-building. It is felt that nation-building should be organised from outside by the community of states in order to boost international security, in particular (Ottaway 2002:17). Questions concerning the democratic ability of the structures created and the role of the population concerned are somewhat overlooked in this process in favour of a rather mechanistic reconstruction of the state concerned or are simply not viewed as a central theme. Understood in this way, we are concerned here with an actual 'building' process, that is the construction of a state or nation.

- At the other pole, nation-building is regarded as an autonomous process of the development of a nation, that is nation-forming, which can only be achieved by the societies themselves and which goes beyond securing a monopoly of force, the ability of the state apparatus to function and the setting-up of infrastructure. The development of a national identity helps the population to grow together into a collective community of will. External actors do not play any role in this regard; exerting their influence would be a disruptive interference in the country's national sovereignty. At best, they could offer support in relation to post-conflict reconstruction, for example (Hamre and Sullivan 2002:89ff).

A further striking feature is that the term 'nation-building' is predominantly used in the debate on foreign and security policy. It has so far hardly been applied at all in the domain of development policy, which is also being increasingly defined via contributions towards strengthening the functionality of the state. The narrowing of these discourses in the sense of a broader understanding of security also makes it necessary to establish a position from the development policy viewpoint. We understand development policy as the area of international politics aimed at helping to shape conditions in other countries on a partnership basis using civil, structural policy instruments and which presupposes that this coshaping process is, in political terms, desired, necessary and possible. Nation-building that goes beyond intervention purely in accordance with international law and/or military intervention would therefore come under the area of responsibility of development policy.

NATION-BUILDING FROM THE DEVELOPMENT POLICY VIEWPOINT

With regard to establishing a development policy position, it would appear meaningful to first determine the object and objective, subject and time frame in functional terms.

Following Hippler in this volume, we understand the *object* and, at the same time, the *objective* of nation-building as being a triad of closely associated constituents.

The first of these concerns the development of a functional statism accepted by civil society. Central to this are the functions of securing a monopoly of force, guaranteeing security for the population and neighbouring countries, the provision of public assets as well as the rule of law and legal certainty, the very functions that define a state.

Second, the building of a nation requires a physical, social and media infrastructure that is shared by the entire civil society. These assets must be accessible to all groups of the population and be used by them for transactions and communication.

These components can be seen as state-forming. Third, nation-building further presupposes a sociocultural structuring and integration process leading to shared characteristics of identity, values and goals. It is not the homogeneity of these characteristics that is relevant, rather the recognition of heterogeneity and facilitating inclusion.

The *subject* of nation-building is the population that together wants to form a nation and assumes the responsibility for this process. Who belongs to this community of will can be determined in the context of a nation of citizens or of origin, though it should be structured as holistically as possible. With regard to the role of the government and civil society, this cannot be formulated any more clearly than in the words of Woodrow Wilson: 'When I look back on the process of history, I see this written over every page: that nations are renewed from the bottom, not from the top' (Wilson 1913). This relates, in particular, to the identity and development of a common political will, which is frequently negotiated in an atmosphere of conflict and characterises the institutional shaping of the nation, i.e. state-building.

Besides this, there are also external players involved in the nation-building process. The emerging nation can directly avail itself of differing degrees of external assistance and it is likewise subject to indirect influence – with this coming from the surrounding states, the international media, plus an increasingly Westernised everyday culture. The emergence of a nation requires, not least of all, recognition and at the very least toleration on the part of the surrounding world – and finds expression in a particularly symbolic manner through a country's admission to the United Nations. This mutual recognition also implies that each nation must make 'sense' to the world around it.

The *time frame* over which nation-building is talked about does not commence with the end of violent conflicts or processes of decline, nor can it be narrowed down to just a few years or decades. On the contrary, there is first an ongoing process of confirmation and further development regarding the way in which the nation sees itself – a large number of examples show that the failure of such confirmation to materialise can also lead to the demise of a nation.

It is this continuous development of an integrated society based on shared values and goals with recourse to a functioning statism and infrastructure that it can also shape according to its own will which we describe as nation-forming in the following. In this way, we make a distinction between nation-forming and constructional nation-building influenced from outside.

HOW DOES DEVELOPMENT POLICY CONTRIBUTE TO NATION-FORMING?

As indicated, external support is also possible and, on occasions, even necessary in a nation-forming process controlled by society. Such support must, however, respect the sovereignty of the emerging nation. It could be argued in this respect that this no longer exists where the society is in an advanced state of fragmentation or the state has broken down and external players must therefore take over the 'helm'. Irrespective of the fact that these players require legitimation through the United Nations, a military operation or the deployment of a force of blue-bereted UN peacekeepers may be able to help stabilise the situation and establish security zones. However, a negative peace – as defined by Johan Galtung – can only constitute the starting point or initial measures for reconstruction and not be interpreted as nation-forming.[1] Although it has proved possible to ensure relative stability in Kosovo, for example, the reconciliation needed between the groups of the population has so far not materialised and protection of the rights of minorities still has to be monitored.

The same is true for creating basic conditions in compliance with international law, i.e. where peace treaties are entered into and UN transitional administrations are set up, it must be ensured that adequate attention is paid to essential conditions like the protection of minorities and sufficient scope is left for the subsequent shaping of the nation. Actual nation-forming can only commence once these requirements are met. This is where long-term development cooperation based on partnership begins. The Brahimi Report[2] illustrates these necessities very clearly.

However, given that development policy is intended to have a preventive effect on a state apparatus becoming dysfunctional or on the waging of violent conflicts, cooperation must be maintained or possibly (re)initiated sooner – even in situations that are becoming increasingly difficult – so as to provide support for reform-minded players in the society and state.

SUPPORT FOR NATION-FORMING:
EXAMPLES FROM GERMAN DEVELOPMENT ACTIVITIES

The following examples of development policy support for nation-forming are not intended as blueprints since each situation requires specifically adapted assistance. Furthermore, the nation-forming process is not automatically helped by every measure that could be classified under this heading. Only the totality and interaction of the three components can constitute such a contribution.

The examples from bilateral German development policy are, as a rule, a part of more extensive strategies to enable bilateral and multilateral players to provide support for partner countries. In the case of demobilisation and reconstruction, so-called 'multidonor trust funds' and programmes involving several donors are employed. Multilateral action can be particularly helpful in politically sensitive regions in terms of 'balancing out' the influence of individual donor policies. In addition to the networking of bilateral and multilateral contributions, the combined effect of state and non-state players is gaining in importance, especially in development cooperation work carried out under difficult conditions.

Statism

The 'democracy, civil society, public administration' domain has become substantially more significant in German bilateral development cooperation activities over the past number of years, with this agreed as a priority with more than 30 partner governments. Added to these, there are a growing number of countries that have selected the area of 'peace development and crisis prevention' as their priority. This means that the political dimension of development is the express focus of attention in around half of the 70 or so cooperating countries. In 2003 alone, an approximate sum of €170 million was earmarked for good governance/participatory development projects. Although most of the programmes are not set up explicitly within the context of nation-forming, their contribution in this regard should not be underestimated.

For the majority of the population, democratic statism is often first experienced as something positive through measures initiated in the areas of decentralisation and municipal development. In Senegal, for example, fostering good governance is associated with the building up of the administration. Strengthening the inclusive element of nation-forming by taking account of separatist endeavours in southern Senegal is also important in this instance. A separate conflict transformation priority to this end has been agreed upon within the context of the cooperation between Germany and Senegal.

In post-conflict situations like those in Afghanistan and East Timor, new structures adapted to the individual situation are being sought in relation to development policy support on matters of statism and good governance for which there may possibly be no example in the nations of the West.

A crucial prerequisite for dealing with these issues is the establishment and safeguarding of a state monopoly of force. Besides support by way of military operations or UN peace-keeping missions, the security sector needs to be reformed as quickly as possible in such a way as to enable the security forces to carry out their task effectively while also protecting human rights, as well as ensuring effective civil and democratic control of the security bodies (Kloke-Lesch and Steinke 2002).

Promoting efficient parliaments that are able to effectively monitor budgetary issues, including the defence budget, is one method of approach. The effectiveness of parliaments also depends, however, on developing an effectual civil society. In many countries, civil society players first have to be made aware of this in order for capacity-building to be able to take hold through non-state assistance and networking measures. The civil society cooperation that has developed in relation to the controversial Chad–Cameroon pipeline shows how such awareness can be enhanced.

Statism must not, however, remain confined to the typical areas of administration and internal security. It is especially the creation and guarantee of basic political and legal conditions in the economic domain that are frequently of decisive importance for nation-forming to succeed.

Physical, social and media infrastructure

Facilitating the economic and social transactions that constitute a nation requires an effective infrastructure. Economic development is central to the cohesion of an emerging society. The (re)establishment of water and energy supplies, the health system, residential accommodation and waste disposal often make up a substantial part of external assistance. The primary task in this regard is to strengthen the government's and society's capacity to act. Where development cooperation supports the provision of public assets, it must be ensured that these are made equally accessible to all parts of the population and that the projects serve to strengthen common interests rather than widen the gulf between different groups of the population. We know from southern Europe, for example, that the readiness of population groups in multiethnic regions to share health facilities with other groups, for instance, can only be built up again at a relatively slow pace.

In Bolivia, the reform of the education system through the introduction of intercultural, bilingual education is also encouraging integration of the country's indigenous population. This provides sufficient scope for the imparting of native values and history. The situation of the indigenous population in Latin America also clearly shows that central issues of nation-forming still remain unresolved even after almost two centuries of independence.

The media infrastructure is of particular relevance for the nation-forming process. In the face of a fragile democratic culture, the media have a large measure of influence with regard to divisive ethnicistic, nationalistic or religious ideologies being reinforced or overcome. The negative examples of the dissemination of hate speeches in the Balkans or Rwanda are widely known. Journalistic ethics and political responsibility on the part of the media can be conveyed through awareness-enhancement measures and a boost given to the media's positive influences. Projects initiated by political foundations, for example, are helping to develop a new media policy which is crucial for reconciling the ethnic groups in Bosnia-Herzegovina and Croatia. The UNTAC radio service also made a valuable contribution to democratisation in Cambodia through a balanced information policy.

Identity, values and goals

As the examples referred to show, it is more often the way in which support is implemented that determines the contribution to the nation-forming process rather than the object of the support. Promoting a shared identity and values is a theme that runs throughout numerous projects. In many cases, the contributions cannot even be precisely classified under one of the three constituent parts.

The support of truth and reconciliation commissions in South Africa or Guatemala, for example, has to be seen both as a contribution against immunity from criminal proceedings and to improving legal certainty as well as providing the basis for a common peaceful future for the different groups of the population, something that is only possible after first coming to terms with injustice, recognition of victims' suffering and reintegration of the perpetrators. Just how relevant this 'coming to terms' process is can be clearly illustrated in the example of Cambodia, where it is assumed that stability and peace will not be possible until the Khmer Rouge have been brought to justice or there has been a public confession of guilt.

The example of settling disputes in an alternative manner shows that shared values and traditions can also be the starting point for creating legal certainty. In Rwanda, for instance, the *Gacaca* lay courts ease the burden on the classic criminal justice system and prevent exemption from punishment, while also contributing towards reconciliation and reintegration by way of traditionally acknowledged public proceedings. In Guatemala, the Konrad Adenauer Foundation provides support in the technical discussion on the compatibility of the Maya law of custom with the state's legal system (KAS 2003:28) while in Bosnia-Herzegovina, the Friedrich Ebert Foundation has supported a series of seminars and radio transmissions aimed, among other things, at recruiting a multiethnic police force (FES 2002: 52). Support for the promotion of confidence building and reconciliation is also provided in numerous fragile and post-conflict societies in the service of civil peace.

This and many other examples show that support for nation-forming in the domain of identity, values and goals primarily begins with improving the possibilities for all groups to participate rather than being initially concerned with culture or civilisation-related subject matter. Although development cooperation can, for example, also help a nation to express identity through cultural assets and historical references, as well as preserving and reflecting on these, the acceptance of a nation by all its members ultimately depends on its being accepted by them in the given context as the best of the social orders possible with regard to intranational and international interaction. Participation is therefore the key concept for identity, goals and values.

DEVELOPMENT POLICY SUPPORT FOR NATION-FORMING – RISKS AND OPEN QUESTIONS

With regard to its sequence and course, development policy support should start with the priority given to those aspects that can be identified as triggering and boosting integration processes and the support of which can be expected to arouse the strongest response among the population at large (Hamre and Sullivan 2002:93). It has to be taken into account in this regard that the players involved can rarely agree unanimously on the priorities – with this being true both for the donors and the internal players. The conflicting coordination processes can have a destabilising effect at an early stage, with the administrative responsibilities overstretching the existing support structures. However, the frequently resulting establishment of parallel structures by the donors undermines autonomy and individual responsibility.

We know from post-conflict situations that a perceptible 'peace dividend' has to materialise quickly in the form of economic and social improvement for the general population to enable the political process to continue. This experience can presumably also be applied to nation-forming. However, this must not lead to the improvement at the commencement of the support phase being induced by an excessively high inflow of financial aid which the countries cannot absorb at that point in time[3] and which, on the other hand, cannot be maintained over the long term, thus resulting in the possibility of people's expectations being disappointed.

In the involvement of internal groups of players, consideration has to be given to how to facilitate social negotiation concerning the nation to be formed without neglecting the relevant social forces. In peace processes or negotiations like the Bonn conferences on Afghanistan, the centre of attention is focused on elitist groups and powerful representatives of the diaspora, who have often formed a government in exile. This frequently leads to inadequately represented groups of the population being overlooked in civil society, with their resulting exclusion impeding or even preventing the nation-forming process. While the involvement of women has gained in relevance (though still low in de facto terms), this situation particularly applies to young, poorly educated men without any fixed income.

In view of these young men, who are easily mobilised and often prepared to use force, and also with regard to former combatants, the tightrope between nation-forming and *nationalism* also has to be borne in mind. Every contribution to nation-forming must bear close examination of the extent to which it can contribute towards a common identity shared by all groups of the population rather than encouraging the isolation of or even discrimination against individual groups.

In conclusion, we would like to once gain point out the danger of *instrumentalisation*. To a not inconsiderable extent, nation-forming is supported and therefore also influenced by the international community on the basis of political, economic and security interests. Development policy should, in a more distinct manner than humanitarian or peace-keeping interventions, only be practised where internal players show a genuine interest in such support and the will to assume responsibility on their own account or where limitations in this regard are compensated for by way of clear mandates from the United Nations.

WHAT PRINCIPLES SHOULD EXTERNAL SUPPORT FOLLOW?

We will now examine – though by no means exhaustively – a number of principles of action, some of which originate from the development policy tradition, while others result from experiences in dealing with civil conflicts.[4] These principles do not apply solely to nation-forming; they are also generally valid for commitment in the context of state failure and the waging of violent conflicts. In all cases, external support should only proceed with the greatest possible sensitivity and only on the basis of partnership.

- In the sense of *all-party involvement*, all relevant groups of players must be allowed to take part and may on no account be selected on the basis of traditional customs or diplomatic considerations. Only action that also includes discourse with Islamic groups, for example, will prove worthwhile over the long term because groups that are excluded will normally look for other – often violent – ways of gaining influence for themselves.

- All sides must be prepared to *communicate* with each other openly in relation to difficult conditions and problems. Cooperation which does not take up the issues of security, structural obstacles to reform, political reservations or suspected abuse of power cannot be effective over the long term. Previous experience has shown that there are not as many taboos as many people believe and all that is often required is to use new forms of communication.

- External support is not free of the *interests* of those who provide it. These interests should be disclosed openly. Measures, the intention of which cannot be made public, should not be applied so as not to undermine the credibility of the external support among the population of the country concerned – or among one's own citizens, come to that.

- Furthermore, the *values and norms*, such as participation, respect of human rights and gender equality, promoted in the context of the support must also be applied in one's own sphere of influence. Non-observance of such standards, for example in cases of corruption in or surrounding development cooperation activities, undemocratic decision-making or availing oneself of sexual services from individuals forced into prostitution, in the course of peace-keeping operations, sends implicit moral messages, the effects of which cannot be underestimated.

- In overall terms, the analysis of the *interactions* between development policy measures and dysfunctional statism, social fragmentation, plus the waging of violent conflict needs to be improved. In the area of crisis prevention and dealing with civil conflict, initial experience is now available in relation to peace and conflict impact assessment, though this needs to be further consolidated, applied to peace-keeping missions and UN operations, as well as extended to include governance, plus state and nation-forming. For example, transitional administrations should be examined to determine to what extent over-hasty political course-setting decisions in elections or constitutional matters make the nation-forming process more difficult.

- With regard to the *sharing of responsibilities* with other policy areas, though also with the sponsor community, greater use must be made of the existing comparative advantages than has been the case up to now. The closer linking of foreign, defence and development policy in the sense of a comprehensive security policy is to be welcomed, but has so far led more to a situation where everyone is doing everything. This results in too little account being taken of experience already gained in the other policy domains. At the same time, work is impeded by the occasional lack of or inefficient coordination instead of exploiting synergies between the respective areas of activity.

INSTEAD OF TAKING STOCK – WHAT SUPPORT DOES NATION-FORMING ACTUALLY NEED?

We have concentrated on the direct contribution of development policy to the processes of nation-forming where this contribution begins with local structures. However, development policy can also exert an indirect influence. Globalisation, breakdown of the state and violent conflicts are influenced by external as well as internal players. These external players can, through trade and economic policies or inappropriate stipulations from the International Monetary Fund (IMF), help create the conditions that make international support for nation-building necessary in the first place. Although breakdown of the state and violent conflicts certainly do not occur because of basic external conditions alone, the deterioration of prices for exports or external shocks caused by rises in energy prices can, for example, bring a country closer to the brink of disaster or contribute to the failure of peace processes.

Support for nation-forming should not first be applied as a cure when new nations are emerging or have to emerge. Development policy can, in part, serve as a preventive measure to counteract the fragmentation, marginalisation and impoverishment of societies, the undermining of state functionality as well as the abuse of power by corrupt elites. Development processes lie in the hands of the respective societies, however. For this reason, development cooperation can only be effective if the corresponding political will exists. Nevertheless, the international community must not turn their attention to the good-performing countries alone and leave the others at the mercy of despotic governments, warlords or attacks and incursions by their neighbours. It must look for non-violent civil means as an alternative to military intervention or simply ignoring 'the blank patches on the map'. The overriding interest of the community of states in inclusive nations with a functional statism as central building blocks for the juridification of international relations and a multilateral order must not be torpedoed by the particular political interests of internationally influential governments and concerns.

NOTES

1. Authors of US origin, in particular, often present pragmatic arguments with regard to dealing with armed, undemocratic forces: 'Whether we like it or not, military power is a necessary component of state-building' (Ottaway 2002:18).
2. The Brahimi Report is the report by the group of experts on United Nations peace missions, drafted in 2000 under the supervision of Lakdar Brahimi.
3. With regard to absorbability in post-conflict situations, see Collier and Hoeffler (2002).
4. We refer here, in particular, to the recommendations of the 'Do No Harm' approach (Anderson 1999).

REFERENCES

Anderson, Mary B. (1999) *Do No Harm. How Aid Can Support Peace – or War* (London).

Collier, Paul and Anke Hoeffler (2002) *Aid, Policy, and Growth in Post-Conflict Societies* (World Bank Working Paper 2902, October, Washington, DC).

FES (Friedrich Ebert Foundation) (2002) *Krisen vorbeugen – Konflikte lösen – Frieden sichern* (Contribution by the Friedrich Ebert Foundation to dealing with civil conflicts. Berlin).

Hamre, John and Gordon Sullivan (2002) 'Toward Post-conflict Reconstruction', *The Washington Quarterly*, Vol. 25, No. 4, pp. 85–96.

KAS (Konrad Adenauer Foundation) (2003) *Konfliktprävention durch Demokratieförderung* (St Augustin).

Kloke-Lesch, Adolf (2000) 'Mitgestalten in anderen Ländern. Die Funktion von Entwicklungspolitik im Rahmen von Global Governance', *edp-Entwicklungspolitik*, No. 14/15, pp. 32–7.

Kloke-Lesch, Adolf/Marita Steinke (2002) 'Den Sicherheitskräften auf die Finger schauen. Der Entwicklungspolitik muss es um eine bessere Kontrolle von Polizei und Militär gehen', *Entwicklung und Zusammenarbeit*, Vol. 43, No. 2, pp. 44–7.

Maull, Hanns W. (2002) 'Die "Zivilmacht Europa" bleibt Projekt. Zur Debatte um Kagan, Asmus/Pollack und das Strategiedokument NSS 2002', *Blätter für deutsche und internationale Politik*, Vol. 47, No. 12, pp. 1468–78.

Ottaway, Marina (2002) 'Nation Building', *Foreign Policy*, No. 132, pp. 16–24.

Rice, Susan E. (2002) *The New National Security Strategy: Focus on Failed States* (The Brookings Institution Policy Brief No. 116, February, Washington, DC).

Rotberg, Robert I. (2002) 'Failed States in a World of Terror', *Foreign Affairs*, Vol. 81, No. 4, pp. 127–40.

Wilson, Woodrow (1913) *The New Freedom* (New York).

12
Nation-building: A Strategy for Regional Stabilisation and Conflict Prevention

Helmut van Edig

This chapter focuses on the question of whether and under what conditions nation-building can have a positive impact on conflict prevention and regional stabilisation. It will become clear that the nation-building process holds both risks and opportunities for regional stabilisation. To understand the interaction between nation-building and regional stabilisation, it is necessary, on the one hand, to take a detailed look at the objectives, contents and players involved in regional stabilisation. On the other hand, the consequences of different variants of nation-building for regional stabilisation also have to be examined. Finally, the question is posed to which extent external players have scope to influence the process of nation-building, what objectives are pursued in this regard and whether any substantial influence can be exerted on regional stabilisation in this way.

OBJECTIVES, CONTENTS AND PLAYERS INVOLVED IN REGIONAL STABILISATION

'Regional stabilisation' appears in just about every catalogue of foreign policy objectives. Industrialised and developing countries, the European Union as well as international global and regional organisations have all taken up the cause of regional stabilisation. In relation to German policy on Africa, Germany's Foreign Minister, Joschka Fischer, declared (2000:3): '... our second priority area is promoting security and stability in Africa. Here we place our faith above all in regional cooperation, which has huge potential for the creation of stability, prosperity and peace.' In April 2000, the EU Africa Summit in Cairo resolved in its action programme: '... we agree to reinforce the continental and regional mechanisms for conflict prevention, management and resolution ...'.[1] The G8 countries drew up an action plan together with the African side that aims, among other things, at promoting regional African capabilities for conflict management and crisis intervention.

Regional stabilisation can be defined as a continuous process in which countries that have a special relationship with each other, through common characteristics, strive in a sustained and peaceful manner to reconcile their interests in order to thus create the conditions for a secure basis of existence for their citizens.

Regional stabilisation is therefore not an end in itself. It first serves its purpose as an instrument with which to establish human security beyond the security of states.[2] The term 'human security' places both the state and the individual at the centre of endeavours to achieve security and stability (Benedek 2002). Regional stabilisation cannot therefore be neutral; rather it must be oriented towards the model of an extended security concept, as well as to the acquis of international law.

The exclusion of force from regional relations is a minimum content requirement for regional stabilisation. Ensuring the sustainability of stabilisation does, however, require shaping of relations through confidence-building measures, cooperation mechanisms and structures in the security and other domains, as well as through integration where applicable. Where there is a network of constructive, forward-looking relations, the risk of disputes and (violent) conflicts is reduced. A striking example of this is the Organization for Security and Co-operation in Europe (OSCE), whose original aim was to resolve the peaceful coexistence of societies with different political systems. Its central idea today is to promote stability and cooperation on the basis of common norms. It is precisely these changed terms of reference of the OSCE that elucidate the importance of the step from stabilisation through coexistence to stabilisation through the positive structuring of regional relations. A similar development could be possible for Africa with the founding of the African Union (AU) and the revival of sub-regional organisations.

There are different players involved in regional stabilisation. Where these are states, it would be rash to equate these with the countries of a particular region, even though the expression '*regional* stabilisation' appears to indicate this. The term 'region' is enigmatic and ambiguous. The large number of possible geographic, political and historical/cultural criteria that can characterise a region can be used at will to make more or less accurate delimitations. Political practice therefore also proceeds according to political and economic considerations of expediency. The influence of nation-building on regional stabilisation depends, in particular, on the interdependence of the states involved. This can be compared to a system of communicating tubes in which any change has a direct effect on the relations in the overall system. The greater its conductivity, the more the system is affected. The conducting elements via which positive or negative changes are transported are diverse. Geographical vicinity plays an important but by no means exclusive role. The common elements of the political systems, history and cultural traditions or ethnic affiliation have to be included as well as the sharing of common natural resources, such as water used by those residing around the same river basin or oil deposits in border regions.

In addition to states, regional organisations can also be considered as stabilisation players. They have the potential to take on responsibility for stabilisation and frequently develop to form important pillars of a region's security structure (Volmer 2000). They do, however, sometimes display inherent weaknesses. It is predominantly political – also security policy – and economic reasons and less a common regional identity that lead to the forming of regional organisations. Under these conditions, many regional organisations have to tackle the difficulties resulting from their heterogeneity and which interfere with their role as regional stabilisers. Regional organisations that include states outside an authentic regional identity risk burdening the endeavours for regional stability with additional conflict potential.[3] The example of the Economic Community of West African States (ECOWAS) shows, nonetheless, that such obstacles are not insurmountable.

NATION-BUILDING: RISK AND OPPORTUNITY FOR REGIONAL STABILITY

Regional stability is based on a multitude of factors. It is, therefore, not nation-building alone that is crucial for stabilisation, even though it plays an especially important role. Disputes concerning borders, natural resources or economic interests and environmental problems can prevent stabilisation or have a destabilising effect. An essential requirement is, therefore, that the states are willing and able to negotiate and enforce peaceful settlements.

Strong states – cornerstones of regional stability

Even though the nation-state is increasingly subject to influences that restrict its sovereignty of action both inwardly and outwardly, it will remain the essential building block of the international community for the foreseeable future (Tay 2001).

Regional stabilisation will therefore also have to be based in the future on the efficiency and strength of the states concerned. Strength is not founded on the state's monopoly of force alone. In general terms, a state can be described as strong when it has successfully progressed through the process of state and nation-building, the essential criteria of which are penetration, identity, legitimacy, participation, distribution and external sovereignty (Asseburg 2002:68, 75). Penetration, in this context, means the demarcation of a national territory, as well as the establishment of the authority of the state, the centralisation of power and assertion of the state's monopoly of force. Identity is based on the integration of all groups of the population on the national territory into the national community and their identification with the state system. State institutions have legitimacy when they are committed to the public interest and there is fundamental consensus among the population on the type of government rule and its priority objectives, with such consensus expressed in a constitution. Legitimacy can be jeopardised by unsatisfactory results relating to the other dimensions of state-building. Participation signifies political integration of all groups of the population through the institutionalisation of political participation, as is the case in a pluralist and democratic system of a state under the rule of law. Distribution is an element of the integration of the entire population into the state system through economic integration. Finally, external sovereignty is the ability of states to participate equally in international transactions (Asseburg 2002:75ff).

The criteria referred to are important in this context insofar as they also form starting points for external support of the nation-building process in the interests of regional stabilisation.

States without nation – nations without state

States that are unstable can set dynamics in motion that can manifest themselves as a peaceful and participative but also as a violent and repressive process, with corresponding consequences for regional stabilisation. The maximum degree of instability is reached when a state collapses. Failed states are now rightly regarded as a threat to both regional and global security and stability (Kühne and Hildebrandt 2001). This is expressed very clearly in the US National

Security Strategy of September 2002: 'America is now threatened less by conquering states than we are by failing ones.'[4]

History teaches us that wars, revolutions, repression or disputes caused by the arbitrary drawing of borders were more often the forces behind state- and nation-building than negotiations and peaceful reconciliation of interests. Attaining the criteria against which the strength of a nation is measured (see above) is consequently very strongly associated with risks of violence.

Peaceful or violent nation-building processes

It is generally regarded as being the case that the fewer characteristics of a strong state there are, the more potential for conflict nation-building has. Participative and peaceful nation-building processes are impeded by the fact that the partial processes referred to reinforce each other to some extent while also standing in contradiction to each other in part. Where it is possible to broaden participation and establish distribution mechanisms, this furthers the legitimation of the state and regime as well as the development of a collective identity. However, inconsistencies exist, among other things, between the stabilisation of state structures and establishment of the state's monopoly of force and unification processes on the one hand and the extension of participation, allowing of pluralism and establishment of opposition structures on the other hand (Asseburg 2002:80). An important basis for the stability of a state order is the voluntary acceptance of a national identity and political organisation of the community, as voluntary cooperation does represent a fundamental condition for lasting unity (Meyns 2002).

The young states of the postcolonial era in Africa and Asia were confronted from the outset of their existence with the problems caused by the nation-building process. The extent of the problems was determined by the initial conditions, which were not identical for all countries. Some states, for example, took over efficient administrations and a well-developed infrastructure, while others had only rudimentary state institutions at their disposal. Following independence, countries of globally strategic interest, in particular, received substantial support, whereas others had to depend more on their own means and resources. A number of countries had become multiethnic states by virtue of the arbitrary borders drawn during the colonial period. Only a small number became independent with a collective identity. All the young states, however, had to deal with the contradictory dimension of nation-building. In most cases, preference was given to penetration and the creation of an identity, at the expense of legitimacy and participation. This resulted in tensions or violent conflicts between groups that were ethnically, religiously, socially or linguistically different. Promises of economic and social prosperity were given which did not, however, materialise in most cases.

The large number of internal conflicts in young African and Asian states clearly shows that no lasting solutions have been found.

Internal and external effects of participative-peaceful or repressive-violent nation-building

Destabilisation as the result of repressive-violent nation-building processes produces a power vacuum which internal and external players are pushing to fill. Internally, the state's monopoly of force is replaced by warlords, ethnic militias and roving gangs of youths who wrest sovereignty over parts of the territory away from the state and implant themselves with their own machinery of power and force (Traub-Merz 2003). The conflict in the Democratic Republic of the Congo clearly illustrates, better than any other example, the effects of a state crisis on regional stability and the significance of access to natural resources as a compelling motive. Besides the 'economic intervention' of the neighbouring states, which compete with each other in this respect, the flows of refugees arising in the region of the Great Lakes and other regions of Africa (southern Sudan/Uganda; Somalia/Kenya) also have a destabilising effect (Kühne and Hildebrandt 2001). Gun-running, drug-trafficking and organised crime place an additional burden on regional stability. Furthermore, ethnic groups that are divided by borders and repressed in a country tend to spread unrest to neighbouring states. A good many of the factors that put a strain on regional stability also have a global impact. The events of September 11, 2001 have shown that extremist movements use failed or weak states as a sanctuary to expand their lawless activities at the global level. The same applies to organised crime, money-laundering and other illegal financial transactions.

OPTIONS FOR ACTION

Regional stabilisation as an essential element of German and international peace policy

The community of states cannot, in its own security interests, adopt a passive attitude towards regional destabilisation. This applies, in particular, to states or communities of states affected by the consequences of destabilisation, such as the European Union in relation to the states in the Balkans or – following eastward enlargement – the countries of the south Caucasus (Ehrhart 1999).

Beyond the security interests, the objectives of a value-oriented policy determine actions and reactions in relation to problems of regional stability. This is true, in particular, for Germany's policy, the central elements of which are to promote peace, stability and welfare (German Foreign Office 2002:2).

Basic conditions for promoting regional stabilisation

It is primarily the states and the political and social forces at work in them that are responsible for nation-building and internal and external stabilisation. Assistance from outside cannot replace the states' own responsibility for achieving these objectives (Niedziella 2000). These can only be carried out in a subsidiary manner where the state and political system has failed. Every outside intervention is confronted with a range of problems. External initiatives and policies related to nation-building have to be in accord with independence and self-determination. Nation-building imposed or executed from outside frequently leads to a new potential for violence.

National identity, as an important element of nation-building, can certainly not be established from outside. Its emergence can, however, be supported by better basic conditions (communication, transport links, schools, economic integration, etc.), which make growing together easier. Subsidiary action by external players is also required where regional organisations are not willing or able to prevent serious and regionally destabilising breakdown of the state or flagrant violations of human rights. One example in this context was the Organisation of African Unity (OAU) prior to the founding of the African Union (AU), whose hands were tied by the OAU charter's rule of non-intervention and which could therefore only look on during the actions of dictators like Idi Amin and Bokassa or the genocide in Rwanda (Meyns 2002).

Multidimensional approach

Despite the restrictions referred to, possibilities do exist to promote regional stability via a range of measures that serve the nation-building process. The prerequisite in this respect is a comprehensive and sustainable approach that takes account of the different dimensions of nation-building. The EU and Germany give preference in this context to civil crisis prevention, settlement of conflicts and the consolidation of peace. The German government's general concept of crisis prevention and the settlement of conflicts (as at 2002) postulated an overall strategy which interlinked instruments from different relevant policy domains. The concept proceeded from the position that crisis prevention in the broadest sense is successful where external and internal players from the state and society concentrate and coordinate their potential for preventing crises. The EU's Göteborg Programme from July 2001 for the prevention of violent conflicts, which is aimed at improving the mobilisation of instruments at the EU's disposal for the cross-sectional task of 'conflict prevention', pointed in the same direction. Even though crisis prevention should primarily be of a civil nature, experience in Bosnia, East Timor, Afghanistan and Macedonia shows that military means can be necessary as an instrument of crisis prevention and crisis management in order to prevent or end the violent waging of conflicts or so as to first create the conditions under which the causes of conflict can be tackled by civil means. Military means must, however, be embedded in an overall strategy and cannot be a substitute for civil measures of conflict management. The peace-keeping operations conducted by the United Nations also have to be viewed from this perspective.

Promoting peaceful conflict management mechanisms that facilitate the nation-building process

Conflicts that arise during the course of social development and nation-building are a natural phenomenon. They only present a risk if there is a lack of mechanisms for peaceful conflict management. The primary requirement here is for effective state institutions, though contributions towards crisis prevention on the part of society are also essential. Supporting and promoting structures established under the rule of law, democracy and responsible governance are important contributions towards the nation-building process in this context. In authoritarian states, as well as in transforming countries and weak or failed states, state institutions can in many instances not be considered as cooperation partners, or only to a limited extent. The task in this case is to identify new partners as well as find new target groups and modified forms of cooperation. Even though cooperation with official bodies can often not be avoided, greater focus is concentrated on cooperation with peaceable forces of civil society, to which non-state cooperation players such as non-governmental organisations (NGOs), political foundations or the churches can add comparative advantages. Unhindered development of the civil society is required to safeguard the durability of the constitutional state and democracy, while at the same time ensuring the assertion of responsible governance and the prevention of corruption. The role of civil society is not uncontroversial, however. It is the mouthpiece of the population vis-à-vis the state and can exert pressure on the latter to take account of the needs of the country's citizens. On the other hand, there is a risk – as in a number of African countries – of state structures being undermined (Kühne and Hildebrandt 2001; cf. Schade, Chapter 10 in this volume). In the final analysis, civil society can only act complementarily to the state; it cannot replace it.

Special attention will have to be given to the establishment of 'peace economies' to supersede the economic base of violent conflicts. The conflict-relevant dimension of private economic dealings is also being included in the deliberations to an increasing extent. The UN Secretary-General's Global Compact initiative is a particularly striking example in this regard.

Safeguarding bases of existence

Integrating the entire population into the state system through economic integration (state's distribution function) is an essential element of the nation-building process. Stability is endangered by extreme poverty, unequal distribution of prosperity and lack of access to resources – coupled with inadequate structures to manage the reconciliation of economic and social interests. The UN Millennium Summit held in autumn 2002 declared its support for the goal of halving the numbers of people suffering extreme poverty by the year 2015, thus tackling a central structural cause of conflict. The German government has adopted the Action Programme 2015 to implement this objective. This programme also strives for structural changes at international level with the aim of establishing a more just and ecologically more sustainable economic and financial order so as to create better conditions for controlling the effects of globalisation.

Globalisation also means that state sovereignty has lost some of its significance in important areas. This restricts a state's capacity to act and a gap emerges between citizens' expectations and the state's ability to react, which can lead to a legitimation crisis that weakens the state (Reinicke and Witte 1999). The loss of a nation's capacity to act therefore needs to be compensated for by improved possibilities for states to be involved in international decision-making processes.

Strengthening the regional relations network

The benefits of regional cooperation are many and diverse – in addition to removing possible hostile images and creating an atmosphere of self-responsibility for the region's political stability, it can also help to raise living standards by establishing bigger markets; this, in turn, strengthens the states concerned. Regional cooperation can stabilise border regions, thus preventing conflicts from spilling over into neighbouring states.

A multilateral approach of this kind is in line with the central objectives of German foreign policy. Increasing the capacity to act and the efficiency of international players in the domain of crisis prevention, such as the UN, the OSCE, the AU and regional organisations in Africa, is therefore a priority objective, the achievement of which depends, however, on global and regional conditions. Seen in global terms, the forming of regional blocks can give rise to rivalries and new tensions. Nor can it be ruled out that the formation of regional organisations will hinder integration at higher levels.

Regionally, e.g. in the Asian context, the scope for external players is less because greater emphasis is placed on the concept of sovereignty, as the following two quotations clearly demonstrate:

> We should ... explore security models that conform to the regional circumstances. The experience of other regions may be drawn upon, but cannot be copied and still less imposed upon this region,

commented Sha Zukang, the Chinese ambassador to the UN in Geneva (Zukang 2000). And the former Indonesian ambassador to Germany, Martodiredjo Hartono (1995), emphasises:

> The Southeast Asian region is the responsibility of the respective regional power. The security system of the region therefore must be 'home grown'. ... Indonesia opposes the dominating roles assumed by foreign powers in Southeast Asian regional affairs, especially in the political and military realms. Southeast Asia should be given a chance to solve its own problems.

There is also an underlying concern here that regional organisations could intervene in internal matters.

In contrast, regional cooperation in Africa has in the meantime taken on a qualitatively different nature with the founding of the AU and the strengthening of the regional organisations. A sense of responsibility for security policy is beginning to develop within the regions and regional organisations, the fostering of which the German government hopes will produce long-term security effects in the sense of the joint containment and prevention of conflicts (Wieczorek-Zeul 2001). It has considerably increased the amount of support for regional organisations and supraregional projects in sub-Saharan Africa within the framework of development policy cooperation (German Government 2001).

Of particular importance for regional stability is the G8 Africa Action Plan, under which partners from industrialised countries and developing countries in Africa have come together to, among other things, expand the instruments of security-policy cooperation in Africa at regional and continental level. The aim over the long term is for the AU and African regional organisations to have efficient institutions for conflict prevention and management at their disposal (German Government 2001). Gravitation centres of stabilisation, like the East African Community (EAC) in East Africa or ECOWAS in West Africa, for instance, are suitable starting points. Individual sectors such as water management in international river basins are of particular significance in this regard. The G8 emphasise, for example, the importance of sensible management of water resources since water could become a cause for conflict in disputes between states whereas cross-border inshore waters can also prove to be a catalyst for regional cooperation once the countries recognise the advantages of this (Eid 2003:58).

The Stability Pact for South-East Europe initiated in 1999 with the priority of reestablishing a network of regional relations is also a model for regional stabilisation. The Stability Pact was a turning point. It has been instrumental in realising the concept of crisis prevention and, therefore, regional stabilisation in a comprehensive approach for the first time in south-east Europe despite the heterogeneity of the players concerned (cf. Reljić, Chapter 8 in this volume).

In conclusion, it can be said that regional stabilisation is a process defined by values, the course of which is determined by the capacity to act of the states involved. The possibilities of external players to exert influence on the nation-building process and regional stabilisation are, however, limited. The essential instruments for action are the promotion of mechanisms for peaceful conflict management and safeguarding the individual's basis of existence as well as strengthening the network of regional relations.

NOTES

1. The Action Programme is available at <europa.eu.int/comm/development/body/eu_africa/docs/cairo_en.pdf#zoom=100>.
2. Re human security, see UNDP (1994) and German Government (2002).
3. An example of this is the accession of the Democratic Republic of the Congo to the Southern African Development Community (SADC).
4. The National Security Strategy of the United States, September 2002 <www.state.gov/r/pa/ei/wh/c7889.htm>.

REFERENCES

Asseburg, Muriel (2002) *Blockierte Selbstbestimmung: Palästinensische Staats- und Nationenbildung während der Interimsperiode* (Aktuelle Materialien zur Internationalen Politik 65, Baden-Baden).

Benedek, Wolfgang (2002) *Human Security and Prevention of Terrorism* (Occasional Paper Series, European Training and Research Centre for Human Rights and Democracy (ETC), 2, October, Graz) <http://www.etc-graz.at/publikationen/Seiten%20aus%20Human%20Security%20-%20Vienna%20Lecture%2010-2002-3.pdf>.

Ehrhart, Hans-Georg (1999) 'Stabilitätspakt für Südosteuropa', *Blätter für deutsche und internationale Politik*, August, pp. 916–19.

Eid, Uschi (2003) *Die Umsetzung des G8-Afrika-Aktionsplans.* Report on the G8 summit held in Evian on 1–3 June 2003 <www.bmz.de/themen/imfokus/g8Gipfel/index.html>.

Fischer, Joschka (2000) *Afrika und Europa: Partnerschaft zwischen Solidarität und Selbstverantwortung* (Berlin) <www.auswaertiges-amt.de/www/de/infoservice/presse/presse_ARCHIV?archiv_id=699>.

German Foreign Office (2002) *Foreign-policy Strategy for the Region of East Africa* (Berlin) <www.auswaertiges-amt.de/www/de/aussenpolitik/regional konzepte/afrika>.

German Government (2001) *Afrika-Politik der Bundesregierung. Antwort auf die Große Anfrage der FDP* (BT Drucksache 14/5582).

German Government (2002) *Gesamtkonzept: 'Zivile Krisenprävention, Konfliktlösung und Friedenskonsolidierung'* (Berlin) <www.auswaertiges-amt.de/www/de/aussenpolitik/friedenspolitik/ziv_km/konfliktpraev_html>.

Hartono, Martodiredjo (1995) *Indonesia in the Asia-Pacific Region: Its Role in ASEAN and APEC* (Occasional Paper 2, Trier) <www.zops.uni-trier.de/op/OccasionalPapersNr02.pdf>.

Kühne, Winrich/Ernst Hildebrandt (2001) *Evolving Global Governance Structures. Division of Labour and Co-operation between Regional and Global Security Arrangements* (SWP study 18/01, Berlin).

Meyns, Peter (2002) 'Die "Afrikanische Union" – Afrikas neuer Anlauf zu kontinentaler Einheit und globaler Anerkennung', in *Afrika Jahrbuch 2001*, ed. by Rolf Hofmeier and Andreas Mehler (Institute for African Studies, Hamburg), pp. 51–67.

Niedziella, Dietmar (2000) 'Umfassender Ansatz. Der Stabilitätspakt für Südosteuropa', *IFDT Zeitschrift für Innere Führung*, No. 1/2 <www.ifdt. de/0001/Artikel/Niedziella.htm>.

Reinicke, Wolfgang Z. and Jan Martin Witte (1999) 'Globalization and Democratic Governance: Global Public Policy and Trisectoral Networks', in Carl Lankowski (ed.), *Governing Beyond the Nation-State. Global Public Policy, Regionalism or Going Local?* (AICGS Research Report 11, Washington, DC), pp. 1–39.

Tay, Simon S.C. (2001) *Comments on Dani Rodrik's FOUR SIMPLE PRINCIPLES.* (Singapore) <www.demglob.de/comments1/tay1.html>.

Traub-Merz, Rudolf (2003) *Afrika zwischen Staatszerfall, Stabilisierung und regionalen Sicherheitsstrukturen: Beispiel Westafrika* (Beitrag zu den Afrika-Tagen der Friedrich-Ebert-Stiftung, 'Afrika auf neuen Wegen?', Bonn).

UNDP (United Nations Development Programme) (1994) *Report on Human Development 1994* (New York).

Volmer, Ludger (2000) *Rede zum Afrika-Tag* (Bonn, 25 May) <www.auswaertiges-amt.de/www/de/infoservice/presse/presse_archiv?archiv_id=>.

Wieczorek-Zeul, Heidemarie (2001) 'Die afrikanische Herausforderung – Eckpunkte einer strategischen Afrika-Politik', *Entwicklung und Zusammenarbeit*, Vol. 42, No. 5 (May), pp. 158–64.

Zukang, Sha (2000) *Some Thoughts on Establishing a New Regional Security Order.* Statement to the East-West Center's Senior Policy Seminar (Honolulu) <http://genevamissiontoun.fmprc.gov.cn/eng/5180.html>.

13

Nation-building: Possibilities and Limitations of External Military Contributions

Heinz-Uwe Schäfer

Operations by multinational armed forces to stabilise countries in crisis regions have considerably increased in number and intensity over the past few years. Of the total of 55 United Nations peace-keeping missions since 1945, as many as 41 of these have taken place in the last 14 years. The deployment figures for the German armed forces reflect this situation graphically: in 1994, only twelve German soldiers – under the United Nations observer mission in Georgia – were stationed abroad as part of a peace-keeping mission. Just nine years later, there were over 8,000 soldiers of the German armed forces taking part in eight foreign operations on three continents – most of which can be classified as military contributions to nation-building – predominantly in the Balkans but also in the remote mountain region of the Hindu Kush.

While political decision-makers worldwide are sending their forces to distant regions to an ever-increasing extent to help consolidate peace processes and promote nation-building, the discussion concerning the possibilities and limitations of external troops in performing this mandate is in its infancy. This also applies to the important question regarding the justification, embedding and objective of such military actions. Recourse to 'international obligations' or the need for 'humanitarian intervention' alone are not sufficient to provide convincing justification for the objective, appropriateness and duration of military peace-keeping operations.

Even though the German armed forces are not involved in what is so far the biggest and most costly attempt by a US-led 'coalition of the willing' to restore security and order, with around 200,000 soldiers in postwar Iraq (an operation that also continues to dominate public awareness in Germany), the current developments in the Middle East should provide additional stimulus to this overdue debate.

The exponential increase in military operations within the context of the multinational commitment to nation-building can be ascribed to two main factors: first, the number of countries whose populations have to cope with the consequences of preceding (civil) wars has risen substantially; second, the interest of the international community in supporting such states in this endeavour – also and in particular through the provision of military forces – has grown significantly.

In order to assess the role of external military contributions in relation to nation-building processes, I will first look at the most important causes for this growing need. This is followed by an examination of the motives of external players for deciding on ever-greater military involvement in the nation-building process.

WORLD ORDER, TERRORISM AND NATION-BUILDING

The spectacular increase in failed nation-building processes or those degenerating into violence that have been observed over the past number of years can, in the main, be traced back to the end of the Cold War. The conflict between East and West had polarised international relations in the preceding decades and, in a certain way, also stabilised them. It was in actual fact the danger of a global nuclear apocalypse that formed the regulative and disciplinary momentum for this global order.

This competition for power and the nuclear stalemate situation subdued critical developments in most cases, even in those regions that could not be directly assigned to either of the two centres of power. To that extent, although this artificially produced pseudo-order was not characterised by peaceableness in the real meaning of the word, it was typified by an enforced stability.

A posteriori, violent eruptions of conflicts predominantly motivated by power politics and ethnic factors, also in Europe, revealed the subduing effect that the Cold War had on the potential for escalating regional flash points – especially in relation to intrastate conflicts. The consequences of nationalist and religious fanaticism, interethnic aggression and violence increasingly threatened to also involve other countries and regions that were not directly affected by conflicts within the state. Unbearable images of human cruelty, growing influxes of refugees and the latent danger of the uncontrolled spreading of instability and lawlessness have, since the early 1990s, intensified the pressure on the international community as a whole to take action.

At the same time, the end of the East–West conflict and the disintegration of the Soviet Union have also released large parts of the military capacities previously tied up in the antagonism arising from the perception of being threatened and in acting as a deterrent. The possibilities for political decision-makers to take action responsive to these new developments by sending troops have therefore broadened considerably.

Furthermore, the terror attacks of 11 September 2001 have led to the realisation that 'disintegrated states' serve, in particular, religiously and anti-West-motivated extremists as a refuge and control centre for the preparation and execution of terrorist attacks, which have reached global proportions. For this reason, weak or failed states have attracted increasing security-policy interest besides the terror networks operating worldwide.

Seen against this background, countries like Afghanistan have also become the focus of security-policy involvement in addition to the centres of conflict in the Balkans, the geographical coordinates of which were in themselves sufficient to provoke action by Europe. The much quoted phrase of the 'defence at the Hindu Kush' coined by the German Minister of Defence was intended to illustrate that the involvement of the German armed forces in the multinational security presence in Afghanistan also directly serves the security interests of Germany and the international community.

SECURITY INTERESTS AND NATION-BUILDING

Military contributions by external players to the consolidation of peace reflect a normative understanding of nation-building in those countries sending such personnel. Their governments are concerned with quickly creating a minimum degree of security in a state marked by chaos and anarchy following the end of military conflict, a degree of security which is an absolute prerequisite for achieving any improvement in the economic, political and social situation. Only when a more peaceful environment has been created can the civil instruments for reconstruction display their full effect.

The conventional, positive expressions of 'peace-keeping mission' or 'humanitarian intervention' relating to military contributions to the nation-building process do make it easier, in their pithy, morally accentuated concepts, to raise broad support from the parliaments and societies in the countries sending troops while, at the same time, evidently facilitating the forming of consensus at the international level. They do not, however, do justice to the generally complex interests of the nations providing the soldiers.

Justifications reduced to ethical arguments fall short as an attempt to brush aside critical questions concerning the main decision-making criteria. The question, for example, of why the international community comes to an agreement on intervening in case X but not in case Y, although the prevailing situation is comparable in both countries, can thus not be answered convincingly in this way, nor by referring to limited military resources. It is necessary in this respect to explain the political motives for intervention more transparently than previously in cases of military operations abroad which go beyond humanitarian aid. It is also quite legitimate and not morally reprehensible to bring specific national security interests to bear in this regard.

Furthermore, the sending of multinational troops should be embedded in an overall political concept for the future of the state affected. Only if there is clarity concerning the final political and military outcome sought can the military leadership establish the role of its forces to the required extent and perform the assignments allocated to it with purposeful prioritisation and adequate rules of conduct.

If this is not done, there will be a risk of the dispatch of soldiers for reconstruction endeavours degenerating into an end in itself and being understood as an expression of the lack of a political concept, while the troops themselves grow sceptical about the meaningfulness of an operation that is, in most cases, highly risky and full of privation for them.

ON THE ROLE OF EXTERNAL FORCES IN NATION-BUILDING

A national reconstruction process supported by external players should, in particular:

- prevent warlike actions from flaring up again (thus creating conditions for supplying emergency aid to the population);
- establish sustainable stability and order, which is a precondition for the return of refugees and economic development;
- protect minorities and returning refugees;
- disarm and demilitarise the parties involved in the conflict;
- eliminate dangerous residues left from the conflict (mines, etc.);

- support the national security forces in the reconstruction process;
- restore essential bases of existence and minimum social standards;
- initiate a new political beginning (democratisation, protection and integration of minorities, establishing basic human rights).

Armed external forces are generally allocated a major role in the first six assignments listed, in particular. Furthermore, their help is also enlisted in the early stage of the nation-building process – in view of the often still fragile security situation – for reconstruction work that is not essentially military in nature in order to bring about visible successes as quickly as possible both for the population locally as well as for the government and the public at large back home. The support of civil projects in the further course of nation-building also helps to increase the acceptance of the troops in the country of operation, thus improving the security of the deployed forces in unstable surroundings. Since 1997, the German armed forces have so far entrusted assignments in the area of civil-military cooperation (CIMIC) to around 1,300 soldiers in the operational regions of Bosnia-Herzegovina, Kosovo and Afghanistan.

Even if the active involvement of the German army and other forces in the reconstruction of devastated infrastructure such as schools and police stations meets with a positive response both among the population in the country in which they are deployed and among the German public, the real motive for sending armed forces for nation-building should not be lost sight of: the aim is to establish a secure environment for civil reconstruction by international organisations and the population itself.

To enable the soldiers to perform the tasks intended for them, they should arrive in the country of operation as quickly as possible and be given a strong mandate. Furthermore, the presence of external forces should be organised in such a way that the process of civil construction can also move forward in the case of a step-by-step reduction of the multinational military commitment, that is ensuring the gradual creation of an environment of self-supporting sustainable stability. Extensive assistance in the rebuilding of national security forces by foreign military experts and police and provision of the necessary equipment should, in addition, help to enable the presence of foreign soldiers to be reduced over time. In practice, though, the picture presented is quite different: in the German army's operations in the Balkans and Afghanistan, there is still no prospect of withdrawal of the troops and soldiers even after a period of eight years in some instances – for example in Bosnia-Herzegovina.

How is it that the deployment of external forces there – and apparently also in Iraq – will probably drag on for yet another few years while the objective of self-supporting stability and, with it, the higher objective of successful nation-building do not appear to be getting any closer in real terms in these countries?

LIMITATIONS OF EXTERNAL MILITARY CONTRIBUTIONS TO NATION-BUILDING

Decisions by the international community, a 'coalition of the willing' or national governments to support a nation-building process are accompanied by particular ideas of the shaping of political, social and economic structures in the country in which the operation is to be carried out. The terms of reference used in this regard relate principally to the situation in the countries sending the troops in order to also ensure extensive compatibility of the country affected with an international system of values and the international economic order in the future. This normative standard, which implies universal validity of a political and social framework based on the principles of democracy and freedom, signifies – especially in countries where the majority of the population has previously had little contact with this system of norms by virtue of its tradition, culture, religious persuasion and living habits – de facto a huge external interference in the nation-building process, especially as it is being accompanied by the weight of military presence. Added to this is the fact that the aim of every operation of this type is to produce success as quickly as possible. This subjects the nation-building process in countries whose populations have just lived through years of violence and expulsion to considerable time pressures.

Besides these normative factors, there is a conservative element, normally expressed at the time of authorising such operations, which also plays a significant role: in general, nation-building is intended to be performed within the old state borders, that is protecting territorial integrity. The important question of whether this fundamental orientation of reconstruction endeavours is the one that most promises success in each individual case is put aside, at least initially, in order to preclude the risk of the state territory being ethnically fragmented and thus becoming a model for other regions.

In an age of civil wars, this political stipulation means in practice that something is to be held together a priori which possibly no longer wishes or is able to belong together. The hatred bottled up inside the population after years of warlike conflicts between the different ethnic groups cannot be controlled by external players. Foreign forces can only help to check its symptomatic actions, such as humiliation and violence. In this way, however, only a superficial and non-sustainable stability is imposed from outside. The state of affairs prevailing in Kosovo and Bosnia-Herzegovina is, in actual fact, a protectorate-type situation, which has little in common with a nation-building process sui generis and serves more to block it to a certain extent.

Even if the deployment of external forces to safeguard a nation-building process follows a well-meaning rationale and – insofar as it has been authorised by the United Nations Security Council – advocates neutrality and even selflessness, the presence of foreign soldiers is often perceived quite differently by the respective populations. The thoughts of atrocities committed by uniformed fighters, still fresh in people's memories, mean that many of them can hardly bear the sight of foreign troops armed to the teeth. On top of this, communication problems and misunderstandings, which can be attributed not least of all to serious cultural differences between the protecting forces and the population, are apt to cause increasing alienation, even if the foreign soldiers were initially welcomed as liberators.

In the nation-building cases of Afghanistan and Iraq, other – extensively identical – political conditions which make peaceful reconstruction and, in particular, the tasks of the external forces additionally difficult also play a role. In both cases:

- the ruling regime was removed from power by external players using superior armed troops;
- opening the state and society up to more democracy and a market economy was defined as the political objective;
- the reconstruction of the countries is intended to ensure that Islamist terrorist groups can no longer operate or be supported from there;
- a national transitional government – or, in Iraq, a national governing council – has been appointed under foreign control to enable the normative objectives to be enforced extensively

in compliance with the relevant interests and, where necessary, against resistance within the population.

The acceptance of external forces decreases in the country of deployment – especially among the political and religious leadership elites – if they are seen as agents of a puppet government installed by foreign powers. If economic reconstruction and the appointment of a legitimised, sovereign government fail to make progress, the growing displeasure of the population is directed principally against the transitional government and the international institutions or national governments behind it.

Added to this in the age of Islamic-motivated terror is the fact that radical groups inside or outside the country take advantage of the fragile and tense situation to further their own interests. They aim targeted terror attacks against the foreign soldiers, who are easily recognisable because of their uniforms, while, at the same time, invoking – also with the help of Arab-Islamic media – the different nature ('lack of faith') of the foreign troops and their negative influences on the cohesion and morals of the indigenous population. Their aim is to mobilise the masses against the 'intruders' and 'occupiers'.

Current events in Iraq suggest that this strategy pursued by a minority of Islamists prepared to use violence is working. The US forces appear, despite their superior equipment, to be unable to establish even the minimum degree of security in their role – confirmed by the United Nations – as the occupying power. There is a danger of their tending increasingly, under the impact of acts of terror and sabotage that can hardly be prevented, towards nervous overreactions, thus causing them to further lose acceptance among the population. The 'open-visor policy' pursued successfully by the German armed forces in Afghanistan has also been called into question following the dreadful suicide attack of 7 June 2003.

SUMMARY

Multinational, military operations within the framework of nation-building are booming. The international community of states should critically examine whether this is the principal instrument that should be employed to create a more peaceful world. Especially in view of what is presently the greatest threat to international security, that is international terrorism, the approach of a cumulative expansion ilitary involvements falls short of the mark because it trains its sights only on the symptoms and not the causes of the increasing tensions between the Islamic and the non-Islamic world. The example of the conflict in the Middle East, which is, incidentally, contributing towards this development to a considerable extent, shows that even a state with vast military superiority is not able to create a sufficient degree of 'perceived' security solely with the deployment of armed forces.

If a number of governments, particularly in 'old Europe', focus more on the question of adequate legitimation under international law with regard to sending soldiers to other countries and call for the United Nations to shoulder the dominant responsibility for such reconstruction processes in order to enhance the acceptance of these operations locally, this is to be fundamentally welcomed. The status of broad support on the part of the international community should not, however, be overestimated. In the perception of radical opponents of nation-building according to 'Western' normative ideas, this does not play a decisive role. These persons are primarily concerned with freeing Islamic soil from alien, un-Islamic influences – at any price.

The (mostly) 'Western' forces deployed in national reconstruction operations – mainly in Islamic states – should only perform a stabilising function in the early phase of the nation-building process and only then where this is absolutely necessary. They cannot replace political concepts designed to counteract disintegration of the state and radicalisation of the Islamic world. It is time to recognise, in a rational stock-taking of the situation, the limitations and counterproductive potential of military contributions to nation-building as well as the need for general political action.

14

Nation-states for Export? Nation-building between Military Intervention, Crisis Prevention and Development Policy

Jochen Hippler

Nation-building in violent conflicts or post-conflict situations is often viewed in most EU countries as a means of countering chaos and fragmentation, as an instrument for conflict management and prevention. Former Minister of State at the German Foreign Office, Ludger Volmer (2002), gave a perfect example of this in June 2002:

> More is needed than the deployment of police and the military to meet the new challenges. What is needed is a long-term political and economic strategy that deals precisely with the forgotten conflicts, failed states, failing states and the black holes on our planet where there is no order whatsoever. Establishing a new state, i.e. nation-building, will become a strategic task for us. Europe has and Germany, too, has an important contribution to make to this end.

The stabilising and ordering function of nation-building is intended to have the effect of preventing crises and reducing violence. This may quite possibly be true, but we should not overlook the fact that some violent conflicts result precisely from aggressive nation-building projects: ethnic expulsions and massacres are frequently intended for the purpose of asserting a particular, ethnically 'pure' version of a 'nation' or breaking resistance against a nation-state government. Other violent conflicts stem from the contradictory nature of two (or more) competing nation-building projects: for example from a policy to maintain the 'nation-state' in a multiethnic context, also by compulsion, or from an attempt to create or homogenise a nation by force, with such an attempt called into question by one or more ethnic groups by way of endeavours to gain independence. While, for example, a Greater Serbia nation-building project would include not only Serbia (including the Hungarian minority), but also the parts of Bosnia settled by Serbs and Kosovo, and relinquishment or loss of any of these regions would mean the failure of the nation-building project, a Kosovo-Albanian nation-building undertaking implies, of course, the independence of Serbia and – depending on one's political taste – state independence or union with Albania.

In political reality, the alternative to nation-building in many cases is not necessarily its absence but, rather, a competing model. Similarly, external attempts at nation-building often conflict with internal variants rather than with a situation of fragmentation, disintegration or lack of rule or government. In Afghanistan, for example, the Taliban and the extremist leader Hekmatyar also wanted to assert their own special forms of nation-building, albeit in a particularly brutal manner. And in many situations, the constructive aspect of nation-building – that is the creation of a nation and nation-state – first requires the dissolution or destruction of previous political entities: the Turkish nation-state was founded on the dissolution of the Ottoman Empire, the Croatian state on the destruction of Yugoslavia, while the Baltic and Central Asian states presupposed the breakup of the Soviet Union.

The development and peace policy discussion on nation-building must therefore proceed from the understanding of the process as the antithesis of the dissolution and disintegration of societies and states, though it should not be forgotten that, in many violent situations, it is precisely the conflict between several nation-building processes that constitutes the core of the problem and that nation-building often first presupposes the fragmentation of larger societies and states. It is thus not always a case of asking *whether* nation-building is taking place or should take place but, rather, *which* of the competing projects is desirable and *how* such a process is to be structured. The significant factors in the context of peace and development policy concern the concrete form of social construction and deconstruction processes, the specific dynamics of the production of ideology related to nation-building (for example joint nationality/citizenship concepts versus ethnic ideologies of confrontation) as well as the policy of the state apparatus vis-à-vis society and the different social and ethnic groups. Anyone wanting to conduct or support nation-building from outside cannot avoid carrying out a serious and precise analysis of the initial situation in order to limit errors and the possibility of failure.

All in all, nation-building does not promote peace a priori. On the contrary, nation-building can, in the initial phase, even have the effect of markedly intensifying conflicts since it is often preceded by a phase of disintegration. The latter may occur because any attempts at integration are rejected by some sections of society, because the methods of nation-building give rise to resistance, or because the losers are able to fight against the unavoidable shifts in power. Even if the threshold of violence is not necessarily exceeded in this context, political and social conflicts will increase for some time and have to be kept under control using sticks and carrots as well as patience. Only when the specific nation-building project is evidently successful and has been consolidated to some degree can a conflict-reducing and peace-promoting effect be expected – this by virtue of the fact that the monopoly of force of a state can be accepted by society and the lessening or better management of lines of demarcation within society can lower the level of internal violence. This positive effect of the second stage of nation-building does not have to depend on whether it has been conducted in a cooperative or repressive manner – even though non-repressive methods are, of course, preferable. Even violent nation-building can bring about a reduction of force over the long term if it is lastingly successful. In this context, it must, however, be ensured that the internal potentials for violence are not simply diverted outwards.

NATION-BUILDING FROM OUTSIDE?

External players now perform a decisive role in the state and administration of a range of countries experiencing post-conflict situations: for example in Kosovo, which is governed by a UN administration; in Bosnia, where a representative of the international community has authority over a complex internal government system decreed from outside; in Kabul, where the president, Karzai, who was installed after the US military intervention, is now supported by a NATO military contingent; and in Iraq, where a US military administration (with nominal British involvement) actually ruled the country and still controls it. External players have also played a decisive role in the shaping of the political situation in other countries, e.g. the US after its intervention in Haiti (1994/95), the UN in the organisation of elections in Cambodia (1993) and the preparation of the independence of East Timor (1999–2002), to name just three examples. The term 'nation-building' was and continues to be used for these and other operations. In most cases, it can be said that it was not the external players that began the nation-building process, rather they only enforced or organised a different kind of nation-building. The reasons for intervention by external players differ greatly: for example as a response to a humanitarian crisis, which leads to the assumption of particular administrative and security functions; interest in regional stability; internal political interests, such as the need not to appear 'helpless' or idle in the face of a crisis arousing attention in the media; strategic and power interests.

In the most far-reaching cases – Kosovo, Afghanistan, Iraq – the external players first crushed an existing power or government system (and their specific nation-building concepts) by force in order to then begin a process of material and political reconstruction, though nation-building was never the actual objective of the respective involvements, rather a means. For example, NATO did not wage war against Serbia in order to carry out nation-building in Kosovo; it did so out of a complex set of foreign policy, humanitarian and internal political interests. After the war, however, there was no other option but to take over the administration itself or transfer it to the UN. The Clinton administration took the way out by reluctantly accepting nation-building but letting the United Nations and the EU countries go ahead with implementing it. In Afghanistan, the political and war objectives of the US and its allies did not involve creating an Afghan nation-state but, rather, smashing the al Qaeda terrorist network, bringing down the Taliban, strengthening their own position in Central Asia and demonstrating their own determination and ability to act after the events of September 11, 2001. After the quick victory, ways then had to be found of safeguarding influence and regional stability and displaying an internationally presentable power model. The poor postwar planning and incompetent implementation of the plans following the conquest of Iraq by the US and British troops were evidence of Washington having prepared extensively for the military action but only very superficially for postwar arrangements (*Washington Post* 2003a).

In Iraq, it was primarily a case of gaining a strategic position on the Persian-Arabian Gulf, bringing down a regional rival and politically reorganising the entire Middle East under US leadership, while looking after important economic interests at the same time. After the end of the rule of Saddam Hussein and the dissolution or smashing of the central areas of his state apparatus, the reconstruction of Iraq as a society and state became a necessity in order to avoid a political vacuum, safeguard stability and, at the same time, promote one's own interests. The first US administrator of Iraq, Jay Garner, had spoken of his mandate being fulfilled within three months and of US troops then being able to be withdrawn shortly afterwards (*Washington Post* 2003b) – a clear sign that nation-building was not the objective of the war. Even after this, Washington still assumed for some time that the number of US occupying troops could be reduced to around 70,000 by the summer of 2003. Only then was it realised that even 160,000 soldiers would not be enough to control Iraq, rebuild it and establish a new political system.

External nation-building is thus often a consequence or instrument of other intervention purposes and rarely the goal in itself – which explains the improvisations, inconsistencies and lack of preparation in many cases. There is not only serious interference in the local balance of power, it also entails a clash of power politics between internal and external players. Anyone who causes inside nation-building projects to fail and replaces them with his own external one has, at the same time, asserted his own power against that of others. In this sense, nation-building also has imperial traits, as Ignatieff (2003) emphasises pointedly in the title of his book: *Empire Lite – Nation-Building in Bosnia, Kosovo and Afghanistan*.

Such imperial undertakings are closely linked to a shift in international discourses – for example to the discussions surrounding the admissibility of humanitarian interventions despite the restriction contained in the UN Charter (prohibition of force, rules of non-intervention, respecting the sovereignty of other states), to redefining (restriction or conditioning in practical terms) the state sovereignty of particular countries or to relativising international law and the role of the UN in general (Hippler 2003a, 2003b).

Imperial variants of external nation-building should not be confused with positive efforts to support internal nation-building processes from outside in the political, economic or security-policy domains. Nation-building can present the temptation for external players to create one's counterpart in one's own image. The Soviet intervention in Afghanistan (1979–89) is an example of this. External players can, however, make extremely positive contributions to nation-building in third countries with different political embedding and greater emphasis on development and peace policy, thus also helping social and political stabilisation over the long term.

However, external support of nation-building also finds itself in an area of conflict between promoting – often contradictory – internal processes and one's own political objectives and interests, which only rarely concur entirely. Internal nation-building, too, is aimed only

Table 14.1   Selected dimensions of external nation-building

Starting points	• Fragmented states and/or societies
	• Failing states
	• Post-conflict situations
Objectives	• Gaining, expanding or securing a position of power or dominance
	• Stabilising a society or state, a government or a region
	• Averting, reducing or overcoming a humanitarian disaster
	• Creating conditions for economic and political development
Functions	• Humanitarian aid
	• Restoration/provision of technical infrastructure
	• Restoration/provision of social infrastructure
	• Economic development
	• Ensuring security
	• Asserting or safeguarding the state's monopoly of force
Necessary or expedient mechanisms and structures and introduction or strengthening of the same	• Capacity-building: strengthening capacities and processes of effective problem-solving in a society
	• State-building: applying capacity-building to state structures, administrations and governments
	• Good governance: the obligation of government institutions to principles such as transparency, freedom from corruption and the rule of law
	• Social integration of different socioeconomic, ethnoreligious and other groups through efficient communication and cooperation mechanisms
	• Strengthening civil society, where not in conflict with the nation-building project
	• Connecting with and integrating partial interests with overall interests
	• Democratisation and elections, establishment of trans- or interethnic participation mechanisms
	• Peace-keeping
	• Military occupation and administration

in exceptional cases primarily at promoting human rights, social equalisation, good governance and participative democracy. As a rule – and this is neither surprising nor reprehensible in itself – its goal is to safeguard or extend the power of particular social and political groups, the positive political objectives of which can, depending on the circumstances, be perceived as helpful or a hindrance. Non-imperial nation-building by external players will also only be able to support the internal project as an overall package in exceptional cases; the components must, rather, be carefully examined to verify whether they are compatible with one's own political objectives insofar as one's own development policy goals should not be compromised. External nation-building for the purpose of promoting strategic interests – including the interest in stability – may disregard this dilemma and, for example, attach greater value to stability than to democracy. This does not make any sense from the development policy point of view. Supporting the nation-building policy of a repressive government may appear attractive to some in foreign or security policy terms (for example the German support of Somalia under Siad Barre as a result of the plane-hijacking by a German terrorist group to Mogadishu; the decades of US support for Saudi Arabia), but in development policy terms it is dubious. This strained relationship between imperial (or expressed more politely: security policy-dominated) nation-building and its development policy variant can also be observed within individual nation-building projects. In Afghanistan, for instance, there is an irresolvable contradiction between the attempts to install and consolidate a functioning nation-state government in Kabul and the US military's close cooperation with and support of local warlords in the provinces so as to be able to use them as auxiliary troops to fight against the remaining Taliban and al Qaeda. This undermines the building of a nation-state (cf. Chapter 6 by Spanta in this volume). Such a contradiction also exists in Iraq in that, on the one hand, the intention is to establish a new political and social system, a new state apparatus and even democracy under Iraqi responsibility while, at the same time, the US authorities want to keep central Iraqi players (for example the Shiite parties and organisations) under control so as not to jeopardise their own interests.

A central and fundamental question in external nation-building endeavours is who guides and controls the overall process. Are the key players the internal government in question or sectors of the internal society (two very different possibilities), is it international organisations (e.g. the UN) or individual external governments (e.g. the US administration)?

Imperial and development policy nation-building differ both in degree and structure. They are contrasting projects which require different basic approaches, different instruments and different use of personnel and resources. Imperial nation-building must, in principle, recreate a nation-state and, in frequent cases, also the corresponding society, even where components may exist for both. The desire to bring this about via external players (regardless of whether it is organised unilaterally or by way of UN policy) is not a sign of political modesty but, rather, an act of creation of enormous dimensions which – depending on the size and complexity of the country and its initial situation – can require substantial financial resources (easily tens or hundreds of billions of euros) and one or two generations of patience. It is particularly personnel-intensive and holds a substantial risk: the undertaking is not impossible but can often be politically or legally uncertain and so complex, so demanding in terms of resources, political will and staying power that failure represents a realistic possibility in the long term (not necessarily in the first few years).

FUNDAMENTAL PROBLEMS OF IMPERIAL NATION-BUILDING

Although imperial nation-building is not impossible in principle, it will succeed only in rare exceptional cases in the twenty-first century. The following reasons for this can be identified.

- *The security problem*: in conflict situations in fragmented societies, the violence itself is often fragmented. External occupying troops therefore have great difficulty distinguishing between civilians and fighters and, because possible resistance does not occur in larger military formations (which could then be fought relatively easily) and is rarely controlled centrally, establishing security is problematic and something for which the military is often not suited. The targets against which the occupiers could act frequently remain in the dark or they are so closely linked to civilians or civilian targets that they can only be fought against if large numbers of civilian casualties are acceptable. This is not only problematic in terms of ethics and international law, but also politically because civilian casualties set the population against the occupying troops and legitimise the resistance. And in cases where some groups in a multiethnic society suffer more civilian casualties than others, the ethnic boundaries are intensified and ethnic identities strengthened and radicalised.
- *The political problem of local rulers and warlords*: since the priority in imperial nation-building has to be placed on military security (including that of one's own troops) and one is dependent upon functioning partners in the country, there is a great incentive to use local power structures, militias, warlords and even criminal gangs as auxiliary troops. In Kosovo, for example, the UN administration worked together with the UÇK militia for some time even though the latter was involved in numerous criminal activities, the expulsion of Serbian and Roma minorities, plus

other activities, including intimidation of the population – partly because of fears of UÇK military resistance, such as attacks on KFOR units. In Afghanistan, deals made with local warlords (through the supply of weapons and money) have resulted in strengthening these elements against the central government and thus undermining the nation-building process. This makes the key objective of a state's monopoly of force even more remote. Alternatives to entering into pacts with local power structures are limited. Attempts to disarm or disband them are often highly risky and require a great deal of time and resources, which is generally unrealistic. In the final analysis, the dilemma of needing dependable, effective and politically acceptable partners with influence in the target country lies in the fact that such partners often do not exist. External nation-building is then left in a state of limbo or it requires even greater commitment and involvement, which can, in turn, easily provoke disapproval and resistance, especially if the internal power factors are circumvented.

• *The question of resources*: in view of tight budgetary conditions and restricted military capacities, military operations have to be limited in time and carried out with the least possible outlay in terms of finance and personnel. This is not always easy: the costs of the US occupation in Iraq at around US$4 billion per month have proved to be twice as high as the amount initially calculated (*Washington Post* 2003c). However, it is precisely this requirement of the deployment of minimum resources in the shortest time frame possible that block the chances of success for imperial nation-building. It may be possible to achieve specific military objectives and realise projects within the space of a few years, but it will hardly suffice for a state apparatus and functioning society to be reconstituted by 'outsiders' in alien surroundings.

• *The internal political factor*: societies in Europe and North America are limited in their patience and readiness for commitment in relation to faraway regional conflicts. Although it is possible to bring about a willingness for intervention in northern industrialised countries by using 'moral' (for example humanitarian or human rights) arguments or fear of weapons of mass destruction and maintain this for a time, keeping it going at internal political level for a greater commitment over 10, 20 or more years with substantial outlay in terms of finance and personnel could be regarded as just about impossible in most cases. Furthermore, there is the obvious problem of internal political reaction to excessive demands at the foreign policy level. The German armed forces, for example, is almost at the limit of its capacity with its presence in the Balkans and Afghanistan, while the US occupation of Iraq is so personnel-intensive that even the US military has been experiencing bottlenecks since summer 2003. It is questionable whether parliaments and the public at large could or would approve a permanent extensive presence or even the expansion of such a presence to other countries.

- *Conflicts of objective and conflicts of objective and means*: in imperial nation-building, there is frequently a conflict between the interest in actual nation-building and interest in control. However, the two require different approaches and instruments: control has to focus on the security aspect because it can otherwise easily erode, especially in the case of external players who are themselves in a precarious situation anyway in the target country. In this context, nation-building becomes principally a means for social and political control of the country and is therefore not an objective but – as already referred to – an instrument for other purposes. This variant of nation-building is shaped according to these purposes, which usually comes down to: (i) an emphasis on military, police and intelligence resources, e.g. relevant support or training of the local state apparatus; (ii) appropriate infrastructure measures, e.g. linking inaccessible areas to make it more difficult to use them as possibilities for retreat or withdrawal and (iii) strictly regulated democratisation and participation possibilities in order to include local political forces in the administration of the country and be better accepted among the public at large without, however, letting go of the reins. An example of this is the sudden cancellation of local elections in Iraq even after the ballot papers had been printed in some cities – a political sign for the Iraqi population of how seriously the promises of democracy were meant by the military authorities (*Washington Post* 2003d). There is also the temptation to use the tactic of 'divide and rule', which impedes social integration. Conflicts of objective and means frequently entail the primary instrument of imperial nation-building – the military – not being particularly suitable for civil tasks of national integration and state-building, while other instruments (for example from the development policy domain) offer less scope for action and have lesser means at their disposal.

All in all, imperial nation-building is a politically and ethically questionable concern which suffers most from the congenital defect of not being able to reconcile the tasks concerning the external control of society with its function of nation-building. The US government, for instance, spoke at length and with joy about its goal to 'liberate' and democratise Iraq, while the US civil administrator in Baghdad, Paul Bremer, stated plainly: 'As long as we are here, we are the occupying power. It's an ugly word, but it's the truth' (*Washington Post* 2003e). The evident tendency of wanting to achieve nation-building in the imperial context a bit at a time, inconsistently, with improvisation, and with the minimum of cost and personnel can easily push such a project to the brink of failure.

DIFFICULTIES AND CONDITIONS FOR SUCCESS IN NATION-BUILDING

Non-imperial nation-building is nevertheless possible and there are many examples of this. Furthermore, successful nation-building can also – after a possible phase of increased instability – make very positive contributions towards stabilising and reducing the potential for violence in previously fragile and fragmented societies. It is not, however, a panacea in hopeless situations; rather it requires appropriate conditions and preconditions, political will, patience, concepts and resources.

The involvement of external players in development policy nation-building in the sense of Hopp and Kloke-Lesch (referred to by them as 'nation-forming' in contrast to 'nation-building'; Chapter 11 in this volume) represents what is still a complex, though more modest and realistic policy variant than the imperial approach. Through its fundamental method of *support* rather than the external creation of nation-building, it limits the risk and one's own commitment, raises fewer political problems or difficulties under international law and avoids the danger of placing excessive demands on oneself as well as hubris. Where imperial nation-building is, in principle, a dramatic act of the creation of nations by foreigners, development policy nation-building resembles, so to speak, the selective drilling of thick timber boards. You can drill the wrong holes or the drill bit may break while you're working, but there's little danger to the workman that the entire house will collapse around him.

Nation-building is not likely to have good prospects of success if – regardless of whether from outside or inside – it is laid over a society like a blueprint. In particular, if an attempt is made to carry out nation-building in the form of merely reapplying Western models to fragmented societies of the Third World – for example a market economy, a democratic constitution and then elections – it will easily run into difficulties, as the example of Afghanistan illustrates. Conversely, attempts to accomplish successful nation-building by pragmatically feeling one's way forward without a sound and workable concept are also problematic in most cases – for example first external security and control, then transferring power to locals little by little. The experience in Iraq points this way.

Like democracy, nation-building also has the best prospects when it fulfils certain functions for the society affected, something which has to be assessed on the basis of the needs of the population and its socioeconomic and political groups. Successful nation-building in situations of acute crises, such as economic and social despair or after a situation of genocide founded on ethnic factors, has much poorer prospects of success than in cases where there is growing scope for distribution and before the complete disintegration of interethnic relations caused by excesses of violence. This applies, unfortunately, regardless of the fact that the need for social and political integration is particularly pronounced in grave conflict or post-conflict situations. The more fragmented a society is and the greater its current experience of violence, the more important control and military and police security will be in order to reintegrate that society over the long term. In addition, the more desolate the socioeconomic situation is and the more this is perceived by the population as being something lasting, the more difficult the internal conditions will be for nation-building.

The question frequently arises in this regard of whether the reintegration of a heterogeneous society is possible at all or meaningful or whether corresponding attempts will only serve to painfully drag out the process of disintegration. Some cases can therefore raise alarming questions in political and ethical terms, such as whether 'ethnic cleansing' can be reversed at all without causing further serious suffering or whether the disintegration of a multiethnic society should be accepted from a certain point and made the starting point of separate nation-building processes, rather than trying to force the different sides into a new entity against their will, like two scorpions in a bottle. This ethical dilemma will often be irresolvable: not wanting to accept brutal excesses of violence and expulsions by taking their results as the starting point for political development, and yet not being able to undo them without perpetuating the violent conflict in a latent or acute manner.

For understandable reasons, the international community has often dodged this question, for example in the Dayton Accord for Bosnia and through the in-between state in Kosovo, where a return of the Serbian and Roma populations that fled or were expelled would set off a new round of violence. A Kosovo-Albanian nation-building process is inconsistent with international law (by virtue of Kosovo continuing to belong to Serbia under international law and on the basis of the Rambouillet agreement), while not taking such action or attempting to assert the affiliation to Serbia would escalate the conflict again beyond the threshold of violence.

STARTING POINTS FOR NATION-BUILDING

Nation-building is a painful, contradictory and complex process which tends to promise success more when the population affected perceives practical improvements in its actual living circumstances and implicitly or explicitly associates these with the nation-building process. If living conditions deteriorate further or stagnate at a low level, the legitimacy of every political project which the population regards as being responsible for this will suffer. A lack of legitimacy could, theoretically, be compensated for by compulsion for a time, though this is not desirable and cannot be sustained over the long term. Nation-building is accepted or at least tolerated when it arouses hope for a better future and there are at least some credible indications of this – otherwise it can easily be perceived as something alien, enforced, artificial or threatening. There is then a danger of the resulting dissatisfaction providing strength for alternative political models (of a secessionist, ethnic or religious nature) at the expense of the integration process.

The new 'nation' must therefore – first – have the feeling that 'its' new nation-state can solve the social problems in the interests of the population, otherwise it will be extremely difficult to convey. A needs-oriented approach of this kind will normally contain economic and sociopolitical components (safeguarding food supplies, living accommodation, jobs, healthcare, etc.) but should not be narrowed down to this. In many societies, matters of personal security (especially in post-conflict situations or after overcoming a repressive dictatorship), corruption, infrastructure (energy and water supplies) as well as cultural symbols and forms of expression are of almost equally great importance.

Secondly, in conjunction with the improvement in the living situation, the necessary politicostructural changes should be implemented, whereby the internal political and cultural conditions must be made the starting point. It is not a case here of a schematic introduction of democracy but, rather, of creating the prerequisites for it, for example a functioning, expeditious and economical legal system, a fair and effective fiscal system that does not favour (especially ethnic) elites, a responsible police force and military that stand above political and social groups, as well as the opening of society to pluralism. Equal access possibilities to an education system that opens up economic and living opportunities is an important aspect in many societies. The rule of law, personal security and equal treatment of all sectors and groups of society are the main focus of attention in this context. All this is, however, easier to postulate than it is to implement since some previously privileged groups will perceive such equal treatment as a loss of power and as discrimination.

The third level of successful nation-building relates to the nationwide networking of the political sector. The reforms of the individual domains must be brought together through integration of the state apparatus (and society) – functioning political sectors are an important prerequisite, though not the core of nation-building. Only when the state apparatus grows into a totality, integrates its components both politically and ideologically and, at the same time, produces political mechanisms for the integration of the different sectors of society or cooperates with them – parliaments, governments, allegiances and their requirements, e.g. functioning political parties, an active civil society or political discourses relating to society as a whole – only then can we actually speak of nation-building. This aspect also includes the legal and actual enforcement of the state's monopoly of force.

The three levels shown in Table 14.2 should not be misunderstood as a phase model in this context; they are, rather, dialectically related. If there is no state apparatus functioning to a reasonable degree, it will hardly be possible to manage the first two levels successfully; and without a certain amount of success at those levels, it will be difficult to make a fragile and ineffective state into an effective one. This is precisely where the core strategic difficulty lies. The complex nation-building process cannot just be executed systematically and in clear stages; rather it can, under some circumstances, quite simply signify the placing of excessive demands on the political and economic structures in weak and divided societies. There is rarely a central point from which all other problems could be easily resolved.

Table 14.2   Three starting points for nation-building

- *Perceptible improvement of actual living conditions*
  e.g. in the economic, social and personal security domains
- *Structural reforms in individual sectors*
  e.g. police, legal system, health and education systems, infrastructure, fiscal system
- *Integration of the overall political system*
  e.g. through national political parties, strengthening civil society, discourses relating to society as a whole, elections and parliaments, balance between centralised and federal political elements

---

It is precisely at this juncture that external assistance can play an important supporting role, as long as it does not succumb to the imperial temptation, by intervening at one or more of the three levels with problem-solving capacities and resources – not in order to replace internal nation-building with the external variety but, rather, to provide the internal players with greater scope so that they do not have to tackle three complex sets of problems at the same time in a situation of weakness. Although the process itself can still only be mastered by the internal players, their chances of success can be increased or diminished from outside. This point can hardly be overemphasised: successful nation-building can only take place when the necessary prerequisites for it exist in the country itself and suitable internal players are available. Pei and Kasper (2003:5) stress, among other things, the importance of a fundamentally effective state apparatus: '... strong performance capability within the state is almost always a prerequisite for success'. Even though this sounds virtually tautological – the building of a functioning nation-state presupposes a strong state – it is not wrong: without basic political and administrative functionality at the very least, nation-building processes lack the important prerequisites. Pei and Kasper (2003:5) are sceptical about creating a state from outside:

> It is worth noting that whereas a strong, indigenous state capacity is almost always a requirement for success, building this capacity may be a challenge

beyond the capacity of even the most well-intentioned and determined outsiders. Effective state institutions historically evolve organically out of a nation's social structure, cultural norms, and distributions of political power. Therefore, political engineering by outsiders seldom succeeds in radically altering the underlying conditions responsible for the state's ineffectiveness.

If nation-building lacks important prerequisites or these are questionable – and these also include economic, social and cultural preconditions – attempts at external nation-building will frequently and more likely have the effect of adding to the destruction and fragmentation. If both exist, however, a well-founded analysis of the internal conditions and players, a realistic concept that integrates the economic, social, political, cultural, security policy and other aspects, as well as money, personnel and a great deal of patience will still be required in order to be able to take advantage of such an opportunity.

The three starting points proposed here coincide with the three central areas of nation-building presented at the beginning of this book (cf. Hippler in Chapter 1): integration of society ('nation'), state-building and ideological integration; they are, however, evidently not identical. This becomes clear in relation to the role of ideology, for example. While it is in fact the case that successful nation-state-building will remain fragile over the long term without ideological legitimation, the forming of ideology would only be a suitable starting point in exceptional cases since, in the absence of tackling the more strongly material tasks, it would quickly be discredited. Such forming of ideology can rarely be promoted from outside and, if so, only to a minor extent. If the forming of ideology were to be at the beginning of the process, there would even be the danger that it might easily develop an ethnic or other exclusiveness in order to achieve mobilisation for an unsound nation-building project through the exclusion of others. This is, in most cases, not a good idea politically if the objective of conflict prevention is not to be abandoned.

SUMMARY

'Nation-building' historically was and still is a complex political concept. The discussion surrounding it moves back and forth between a rather arbitrary use of the term to describe eclecticist political elements (in the domains of peace-keeping, state-building, reconstruction, occupation politics and the political structuring of outside societies), an imperial variant of interest politics for controlling outside societies and a development and peace policy approach for the purpose of stabilisation and conflict prevention in current and potential crisis countries. The latter offers opportunities to deal with difficult and conflict-intensifying situations constructively insofar as the objective and subjective conditions permit in the individual case concerned. Nation-building in this context is not a miracle cure or any basically new or original development, foreign, security or peace policy approach; rather it represents a possibility of integrating different political instruments and methods in a conceptional manner. Old and new instruments and policies are reevaluated from the standpoint of strengthening political and social integration and combined in order to thus enhance internal development possibilities and the potential for reducing violence.

Such a policy of providing external support for internal, authentic nation-building processes can, in this way, have the effect of promoting development and peace. It does not attempt to reinvent the wheel or simply transfer its own models to fragmented Third World countries – a fault of the corresponding discussions conducted in the 1950s and 1960s; the purpose is, rather, to precisely adapt the set of existing policies and instruments to a politically central domain and integrate them. Bringing these together at a time of numerous and, in themselves, logical 'sectoral policies' and developing criteria and conceptions to define their relation, weighting and final overall objective is a task that needs to be carried out urgently. The integration of fragmented societies and the functionality of a state apparatus corresponding to and serving the society are, indeed, two key strategic starting points that can systematise and facilitate the pursuance of a large number of general and often somewhat more obscure political objectives (development, peace, good governance, etc.).

There are so far only initial signs of an active, supportive policy of nation-building, though hardly perceptible beneath a mountain of rhetoric and incomplete work. It is, however, worthwhile to continue working on this starting point and formulate manageable, unified political concepts – as long as it proves possible beforehand to reject the instrumentalisation of nation-building to make it a technique for imperial power.

REFERENCES

Hippler, Jochen (2003a) 'USA und Europa: unterschiedliche Sicherheitspolitiken', in Development and Peace Foundation, *Globale Trends 2004/2005. Fakten, Analysen, Prognosen* ed. by Ingomar Hauchler, Dirk Messner and Franz Nuscheler (Frankfurt/M.).

Hippler, Jochen (2003b) 'US-Dominanz und Unilateralismus im internationalen System – Strategische Probleme und Grenzen von Global Governance', in Jochen Hippler and Jeanette Schade, *US-Unilateralismus als Problem von internationaler Politik und Global Governance* INEF Report 70 (Duisburg) <http://inef.uni-duisburg.de/page/documents/Report70.pdf>.

Ignatieff, Michael (2003) *Empire Lite – Nation-Building in Bosnia, Kosovo and Afghanistan* (London).

Pei, Minxin and Sara Kasper (2003) *Lessons from the Past: The American Record on Nation Building,* Carnegie Endowment for International Peace, Policy Brief 24 (Washington, DC)

Volmer, Ludger (2002) *New International Security Situation* – Plenary address by Minister of State Volmer at the 4th ASEM Foreign Ministers' Meeting, 7 June (Madrid) <www.auswaertiges-amt.de/www/de/ausgabe_archiv?archiv_id=3254>.

Washington Post (2003a) 'Wolfowitz Concedes Iraq Errors', *Washington Post,* 24 July, p. A01.

Washington Post (2003b) 'Reconstruction Planners Worry, Wait and Evaluate', *Washington Post,* 2 April, p. A01.

Washington Post (2003c) 'Military Operations in Iraq Cost Nearly $4 Billion a Month', *Washington Post,* 10 July, p. A24.

Washington Post (2003d) 'Occupation Forces Halt Elections throughout Iraq', *Washington Post,* 28 June, p. A20.

Washington Post (2003e) 'The Final Word on Iraq's Future – Bremer Consults and Cajoles, but in the End, He's the Boss', *Washington Post,* 18 June, p. A01.

Notes on the Contributors

Claudia Derichs is Assistant Professor at the Institute of Political Sciences, University of Duisburg-Essen, focusing on democratisation and political Islam in South-East Asia, nation-building in multiethnic states and the politics of Japan. Her publications include: *Japans Neue Linke* (Hamburg, 1995); (ed.), *Soziale Bewegungen in Japan* (Hamburg, 1998); (ed.), *Die politischen Systeme Ostasiens* (Opladen, 2003); plus numerous contributions on the region of South-East Asia in German and international book publications and journals.

Helmut van Edig is a former Ambassador; he has been working as editor, publicist and translator since 2000; head of the team set up by the Federal Foreign Office to draw up the German government's action plan on the 'Prevention of Civil Crises, Settlement of Conflicts and Consolidation of Peace'. Publications include: (coordinator/editor), *Crisis Prevention – Conflict Resolution – Peacekeeping* (Contributions by the Friedrich Ebert Foundation on Civil Conflict Transformation, Berlin, 2003); former editor of *Entwicklungspolitische Informationen* (discontinued in 2001).

Wolfgang Heinrich studied Cultural Anthropology, Culture and Personality Research and Linguistics at the Georg-August University in Göttingen and the University of California at Berkeley; worked in Somalia 1995/96 for the Swedish Life and Peace Institute (LPI); from 1998 to 2000 and since 2002: Head of the 'Desk for Peace and Conflict Management Issues' (AsFK) of the Churches' Development Service (EED); in 2001, coordinator of the 'Local Capacities For Peace-Project' initiated by the Collaborative for Development Action (CDA), USA. Publications include: *Building the Peace. Experiences of Collaborative Peacebuilding in Somalia 1993–1996* (Life and Peace Institute-LPI, Uppsala, 1997); 'Building Structures for Self-Determination And Inter-Community Co-operation in Times of Violent Conflict', in Hartmut Quehl (ed.), *Living in Wartimes – Living in Post-Wartimes* (Felsberg, 2002), pp. 265–78; 'There Is No Blueprint For Peace', *D+C*, Vol. 44, No. 1 (2003).

Jochen Hippler is a political scientist at the University of Duisburg-Essen (Germany) and its Institute for Development and Peace (INEF). Publications include: (ed. with Thomas Fues), *Globale Politik – Entwicklung und Frieden in der Weltgesellschaft. Festschrift für Franz Nuscheler* (Bonn, 2003); (ed. with Andrea Lueg), *Feindbild Islam – oder Dialog der Kulturen* (Hamburg, 2002); 'US-Dominanz und Unilateralismus im internationalen System – Strategische Probleme und Grenzen von Global Governance', in Jochen Hippler and Jeanette Schade, *US-Unilateralismus als Problem von internationaler Politik und Global Governance* (INEF Report 70, Duisburg, 2003). www.Jochen-Hippler.de

Ulrike Hopp studied Economic Sciences at the Free University of Berlin; since 1997 with the German Ministry for Economic Cooperation and Development (BMZ); since 2002 with Unit 210, 'Peace-Building and Crisis Prevention'; member of the Interinstitutional Working Group on Peace Development (FriEnt).

Adolf Kloke-Lesch studied Urban and Regional Planning at the Technical University of Berlin; since 1978 with the German Ministry for Economic Cooperation and Development (BMZ), Deputy Director General for 'Peace and Democracy, Human Rights, United Nations'. Publications include: (with Marita Steinke), 'Den Sicherheitskräften auf die Finger schauen. Der Entwicklungspolitik muss es um eine bessere Kontrolle von Polizei und Militär gehen', *E+Z*, Vol. 43, No. 2 (2002), pp. 44–7; (with Hans-Peter Baur), 'Friedensentwicklung und Krisenprävention als Strategieelemente der Entwicklungspolitik', in Tilman Evers (ed.), *Ziviler Friedensdienst* (Leverkusen, 2000), pp. 189–98; 'Mitgestalten in anderen Ländern. Die Funktion von Entwicklungspolitik im Rahmen von Global Governance', *edp-Entwicklungspolitik*, No. 14/15 (2000), pp. 32–7.

Manfred Kulessa studied Law and History in Marburg, Frankfurt and Athens, OH; has worked in the fields of academic exchange, development service and international cooperation, and also as Director in the United Nations Development Programme (UNDP) and UN Coordinator in China. Publications include: (with Khalid Malik), *Sharing New Ground in Post-Conflict Situations – The Role of UNDP in Reintegration Programmes* (UNDP, New York, 2000); (ed. with Rafeeuddin Ahmed and Khalid Malik), *Lessons Learned in Crises* *and Post-Conflict Situations – The Role of UNDP in Reintegration and Reconstruction Programmes* (UNDP, New York, 2002).

Cyril I. Obi is Senior Research Fellow at the Nigerian Institute of International Affairs in Lagos; from 1999 to 2000 Guest Fellow at St. Antony's College, Oxford; editor of the *Nigerian Journal of International Affairs*. Publications include: *The Changing Forms of Identity Politics in Nigeria under Economic Adjustment: The Case of the Oil Minorities of the Niger Delta* (Nordiska Afrikainstitutet, Research Report 119, Uppsala, 2001); 'Ethnic Minority Agitation and the Spectre of National Disintegration', in Toyin Falola (ed.), *Nigeria in the Twentieth Century* (Durham, NC, 2002); 'Oil and the Politics of Transition in Nigeria', in Browne Onuoha and M.M. Fadakinte (eds), *Transition Politics in Nigeria 1970–1999* (Lagos, 2002).

Joanna Pfaff-Czarnecka is a Professor of Social Anthropology at the University of Bielefeld; from 1996 to 1998 President of the Swiss Society of Social Anthropology; presently spokesperson for the Section 'Developmental Sociology and Social Anthropology' at the German Sociological Association. Publications include: (ed. with D. Gellner und J. Whelpton), *Nationalism and Ethnicity in a Hindu Kingdom: The Cultural Politics in Contemporary Nepal* (Amsterdam, 1997); (ed. with A. Nandy, D. Rajasingham and T. Gomez), *Ethnic Futures, State and Identity in Four Asian Countries* (New Delhi, 1999).

Dušan Reljić studied Journalism and Communication, Theory of Politics and Philosophy in Vienna; from 1996 to 2000 Fellow and subsequently Head of Department of Media and Democracy at the European Media Institute in Düsseldorf; since 2001 Fellow at the German Institute for International and Security Affairs (SWP), Berlin. Publications include: *Serbien in Zeitnot. Neuanfang nach 42 Tagen Ausnahmezustand?* (SWP Study 18, May 2003); 'Das politische System der Bundesrepublik Jugoslawien', in Wolfgang Ismayr (ed.), *Die politischen Systeme Osteuropas* (Opladen, 2002); 'Der Vormarsch der Megamedien und die Kommerzialisierung der Weltöffentlichkeit', in Tanja Brühl et al. (ed), *Die Privatisierung der Weltpolitik* (Series ONE World 11, Bonn, 2001); 'The News Media and the Transformation of Ethnopolitical Conflicts', in *The Berghof Handbook for Conflict Transformation* (Berghof Research Center for Constructive Conflict Management, Berlin, 2000).

Jeanette Schade is presently Fellow at the Institute for Development and Peace (INEF) in Duisburg. Publications include: *'Zivilgesellschaft'* – *Überblick über eine vielschichtige Debatte* (INEF Report 59, Duisburg, 2002); 'Unilaterales US-Handeln im mulitlateralen Kontext – Eine tabellarische Übersicht', in Jochen Hippler and Jeanette Schade, *US-Unilateralismus als Problem von internationaler Politik und Global Governance* (INEF Report 70, Duisburg, 2003).

Heinz-Uwe Schäfer is a naval Commander; Business School Graduate; Course Director of the 2003 admiral staff officer course at the German Armed Forces' Command and Staff College. Publication: (with Ernst-Christoph Meier and Richard Rossmanith), *Wörterbuch zur Sicherheitspolitik – Deutschland in einem veränderten internationalen Umfeld* (Hamburg, 2002).

Rangin Dadfar Spanta studied Jurisprudence and Political Science at the Universities of Kabul and Ankara; took a doctorate at the RWTH in Aachen; Head of the Third World Forum Aachen; Lecturer in the Department of Political Science at the RWTH in Aachen; spokesman for the 'Alliance for Democracy in Afghanistan'. Publications include: *Afghanistan, Entstehung der Unterentwicklung, Krieg und Widerstand* (Frankfurt/M., 1993); plus numerous articles and interviews on development, peace, fundamentalism and Afghanistan in German, Turkish and Farsi.

Rainer Tetzlaff is Professor in the Department of Political Science at the University of Hamburg, Member of the Board of Trustees of the Institute for Peace Research and Security Policy in Hamburg (IFSH). Publications include: 'Afrika als Teil der Vierten Welt – der Welt der erodierenden Staatlichkeit – abgeschaltet von der Globalisierung?', in Hans Küng and Dieter Senghaas (eds), *Ein neues Paradigma internationaler Beziehungen? Ethische Herausforderungen für die Gestaltung der Weltpolitik* (Munich, 2003); 'Politisierte Ethnizität als Kehrseite politischer Partizipation in unsicheren Zeiten. Erfahrungen aus Afrika', *WeltTrends*, No. 38 (spring 2003), pp. 11–30; 'Zur Renaissance der politischen Parteien und Parteienforschung in Afrika', *Afrika Spektrum*, No. 37 (2002), pp. 239–57.

Index

Compiled by Sue Carlton